Growing
HEALTHY
Churches

JONATHAN LAMB

Growing
HEALTHY
Churches

Urgent biblical priorities
for local congregations

2022

Copyright © Jonathan Lamb 2022

First published 2022 by Partnership UK (Ltd)
Abbey Court, Cove, Tiverton, Devon, UK

26 25 24 23 22 / 7 6 5 4 3 2 1

The right of Jonathan Lamb to be identified as the author of this work has been
asserted by him in accordance with the Copyright, Designs and Patents Act 1988

All Bible quotations in this book are from the NIV 2011, unless otherwise indicated.

British Library Cataloguing in Publication Data
A catalogue record of this book is available from the British Library

ISBN 978-1-9160130-9-4

Cover design and typesetting by projectluz.com

Printed and bound in the UK by Bell & Bain

Contents

Introduction

E very springtime, some small miracles take place outside our house. We have an area of gravel made up of small stones, over which people walk and our car is driven. It is bare throughout the winter. Yet early in March, small primroses push through the barrier, transforming the lifeless space with bright yellow and green splashes of growth. We have all seen small plants emerging in the cracks of pavement, eventually pushing the concrete aside; we have seen unpromising saplings emerge into fruitful trees. We have all witnessed the miracle of growth from a new-born baby to an energetic teenager. These profound evidences of growth tend to be things we take for granted, but they are each a remarkable testimony to the nature and power of healthy growth.

When we discuss the subject of church growth, it is likely that our first thought relates to numbers. And there's no doubt that this is a significant expectation in Scripture, and an urgent priority for churches too. The book of Acts is a narrative of sustained numerical growth, both of believers and of congregations:

> . . . about three thousand were added to their number that day. (Acts 2: 41)

> . . . more and more men and women believed in the Lord and were added to their number. (Acts 5: 14)

> The number of disciples in Jerusalem increased rapidly, and a large number of priests became obedient to the faith. (Acts 6: 7)

> Then the church throughout Judea, Galilee and Samaria enjoyed a time of peace. It was strengthened. Living in the fear of the Lord and encouraged by the Holy Spirit, it increased in numbers. (Acts 9: 31)

1

> So the churches were strengthened in the faith and grew daily in numbers. (Acts 16: 5)

We long for such growth in our own nations, as the Lord provokes us to a greater commitment to evangelism and church planting. By God's grace, the churches in the continent of Europe, for so long experiencing decline, are now seeing evidence of new church planting initiatives, of growth in lively diaspora churches, and new congregations emerging in previously resistant countries. Globally, of course, we rejoice in the phenomenal growth of congregations in the Majority World of Africa, Asia and Latin America. Christians are part of the fastest growing family on the planet.

Yet in Scripture there is another fundamental expectation: church growth must be qualitative as well as quantitative. Again, we find this concern in the early churches. Apostolic missionary activity was not restricted to preaching the gospel and winning converts. They returned time and again to cities where churches had been planted in order to nurture disciples and bring congregations to maturity. The New Testament letters are specially concerned with this kind of growth, including:

- growth in love (Eph. 4: 16; Phil. 1: 9; 1 Thess. 3: 12; 1 Peter 1: 22; 2: 17; 3: 8; 4: 8)
- growth in holiness (2 Cor. 3: 18; Eph. 5: 27; 1 Thess. 3: 13)
- growth in understanding and experience of the truth (Col. 1: 28–2: 7)
- growth in knowledge of God (Col. 1: 9–12; 2 Peter 3: 18)
- growth in generosity (2 Cor. 8 & 9)
- growth in prayer for the cause of mission (Rom. 15: 30; Col. 4: 12, 13; 1 Tim. 2: 1–8)

The letter to the Hebrews is particularly concerned to encourage growth, with its exhortations to 'go on to maturity' (Heb. 6: 1). The word is also used by James as he urges Christians to display Christlike character: 'Let perseverance finish its work so that you may be mature and complete, not lacking anything.' (Jas. 1: 4)

It was a privilege for me to participate in the fourth International Training Consultation held at Emmaus College in Dubuque, Iowa, USA, in 2018, when we examined the theme of 'Growing Healthy Churches'. Organized by the Brethren Training Network, it was attended by an impressive group of Christian leaders and trainers from many parts of the world. The chapters which follow arise from Bible expositions which I gave at that event, and I am most grateful for the invitation and encouragement of Dr Neil Summerton to put them into print.

The first three chapters are based on the Bible expositions given at the Consultation, and chapter 4 is based on a seminar held at the event. At the request of Partnership, I have also added a final chapter on the matter of Growth and Change, considerably modified from a small Partnership booklet published 25 years ago.[1] This chapter seemed to be a useful addition to this volume. I have written on this topic in a recent book entitled *Essentially One: striving for the unity God loves*[2], and I am grateful to the publisher for permission to reproduce some sections in this chapter.

At the close of each chapter, there is a series of comments and questions which I hope will strengthen application. It may be possible for leaders, or other groups in the local church, to explore these questions together, relating each chapter to their own context.

Inevitably, the themes are very selective and there are many aspects of healthy growth which are not tackled in this short volume, including those related to numerical growth. But it would be true to say that growth in these areas—in spiritual life, Christlike character, Christian understanding, practical godliness, commitment to the truth, and Christian unity—will result in congregations which provide attractive evidence of the truth of the gospel, and which are evangelistically engaged and missionally fruitful.

---

1. Jonathan Lamb, *Making Progress in Church Life: how to handle change positively* (Carlisle: Paternoster Periodicals for Partnership, 1997), available digitally at https://fliphtml5.com/bookcase/thfvr.
2. Jonathan Lamb, *Essentially One: striving for the unity God loves* (London: IVP, 2020).

Such healthy churches will be productive in all kinds of ways, not least in numerical growth.

Of course, the idea of growing healthy churches could be reduced to a mere exhortation to self- effort and organizational reform, and so it is vital that we hold in our minds that, while energetic commitment is certainly called for on our part, all growth is God-given. In writing to address immaturity in the church at Corinth, Paul reminds us that we are utterly dependent on God:

> While energetic commitment is certainly called for on our part, all growth is God-given

> I planted the seed, Apollos watered it, but God has been making it grow. So neither the one who plants nor the one who waters is anything, but only God, who makes things grow. The one who plants and the one who waters have one purpose, and they will each be rewarded according to their own labour. For we are fellow workers in God's service; you are God's field, God's building. (1 Cor. 3: 6–9)

Both quantitative and qualitative growth are marks of healthy churches, and perhaps both are captured in the lovely thanksgiving expressed by Paul when writing to the Colossians. It was very encouraging for those of us gathered at the Dubuque Consultation to witness a contemporary example of what Paul described:

> In the same way, the gospel is bearing fruit and growing throughout the whole world—just as is has been doing among you since the day you heard it and truly understood God's grace. (Col. 1: 6)

Our hope is that this volume will contribute in some small way to the sustained, healthy growth of our churches worldwide, and therefore to the greater glory of the Lord of the Church.

CHAPTER 1

Growth in Christ

Base passage: Colossians 1: 28–2: 7

One of the joys of living in Oxford is that we receive something in the region of seven million visitors each year. The city has a love-hate relationship with these many tourists. On the one hand, the local economy benefits a great deal, as they inject some £780 million annually. But on the other, the streets are crowded, the traffic congested, and the Coke cans and McDonalds' wrappers accumulate in the parks.

Tourists have a particular way of looking at life. They glide into town in their air-conditioned buses, they stay for a few hours, and then they are on to the next city. The tourist is quite different from the pilgrim: the tourist looks for the immediate, the pilgrim for the long term. One is quick and efficient, the other endures hard slog.

The tourist mentality stands in contrast to the New Testament emphasis on the disciple. The disciple is committed to continue, to the long haul, to patient growth, to continual learning. At least, that's how it should be. But for many people, the Christian life can be reduced to little more than a weekly visit to church. We have put our trust in Christ, we belong to the Christian community, but our expectations of change can be very limited.

Worse still, there are many Christians who, having made a good start, fail to continue. Distracted by other things, they gradually marginalise their commitment to Christ and their Christian life, so that it becomes an accessory rather than the driving force of their life.

Growth in Christ

One of the core themes of the letter to the Colossians is the call to *continue in Christ*.

> . . . If you continue in your faith, established and firm, not moved from the hope held out in the gospel. (Col. 1: 23)

> He is the one we proclaim, admonishing and teaching everyone with all wisdom, so that we may present everyone fully mature in Christ. (Col. 1: 28)

> Just as you received Christ Jesus as Lord, continue to live your lives in him . . . (Col. 2: 6)

We know that one reason for Paul's letter to the Colossians was to combat false teaching which was in danger of influencing the believers, part of which was the supposed new spiritual freedom which certain teachers were seeking to introduce. In fact, Paul accuses such preachers of actually trying to capture believers for what would become a new form of slavery. 'Don't let anyone kidnap you', he says (Col. 2: 8). Don't let them take you captive.

The young Christians to whom Paul was writing were in danger of turning away from the truth of the gospel, and turning towards human traditions, rather than the liberating realities of what Christ had done for them. It's no wonder that the letter is full of encouragements, underlining that Jesus Christ is all you need. He is your life and, since you are complete in him, it's vital that you *continue in him*.

So, in the opening verses of chapter 2, we can see that this is basic to Paul's pastoral strategy:

> My goal is that they may be encouraged in heart and united in love,
> so that they may have the full riches of complete understanding . . .
> (Col. 2: 2)

Paul's purpose is to encourage growth to maturity, to completion—to what he calls complete understanding. And he defines this in the next verse:

. . . in order that they may know the mystery of God, namely, Christ, in whom are hidden all the treasures of wisdom and knowledge. (Col. 2: 2, 3)

The whole chapter focuses on the fact that there is no need to look elsewhere, other than to the one whom they already know and to whom they belong. They can have complete understanding in Christ. In him they will discover all that is good, wise and true. For sure, there is a long way to go in exploring the riches of that inheritance, but they should not be distracted. They should not be enticed by fine-sounding arguments (Col. 2: 4), nor deceived by alternative offers of spiritual satisfaction. Paul is insistent: Jesus is enough.

> **Paul is insistent: Jesus is enough**

We know that this is God's purpose for all believers, and this is urgently needed for our churches—we long to see the growth to maturity in Christ, both of believers and congregations.

Our context

When we reflect on the growth of the church globally, most of us have mixed emotions. On the one hand, there is fantastic growth. One of the most significant issues in mission today concerns the shift in the centre of gravity of the global church. In the mid twentieth century, about 75% of the world's Christians lived in Europe and North America. Now the growth in the Global South is so substantial that 75% of the world's Christians are found in the Majority World of Africa, Asia and Latin America, with just 25% (and decreasing) in the North. It is hugely encouraging to see that, throughout the Majority World, there is evidence of large numbers of people coming to faith in Christ. It is a spiritual movement of immense proportions.

But there is another side to the story. For many years I worked with Langham Partnership, which grew out of a concern of John Stott about the wellbeing of the Majority World churches. He frequently asked church leaders what was the number-one challenge their churches were facing. Almost always he received the same reply: 'it is growth without depth.' That is, numerical growth without an accompanying spiritual maturity.

The theologian Jim Packer once spoke on the subject of the importance of the Bible, and introduced his sermon by talking about the redwoods in northern California. He explained that, if you've had the opportunity to visit these magnificent trees, you will have noticed that they are carefully fenced off, and that's because they have a very shallow root system. So as more and more visitors march round these huge trees, the soil is loosened around the roots and they become very vulnerable. In fact, it wouldn't take too much wind to topple them.

Packer then went on to comment that, although there have been many signs of growth in the evangelical church, there is also an unmistakeable shallowness. It's true in the West, just as it is true in the Majority World. In country after country, the story is the same: the church is widely spread, but it is 'thin'. Often, there is limited evidence of committed discipleship and Christian maturity, and this inevitably raises concerns about healthy growth and therefore about sustainability.

Amongst missiologists, there is some debate about the exact definition of mission, but many would agree that what really matters is clarity about the 'ends of evangelism'. That is, mission is not simply seeking conversions to Christ, but also the maturity of Christian disciples and the establishment of stable new Christian communities. This is well expressed in a helpful book on the biblical theology of mission:

> If the apostolic model is to be followed by missionaries in the con-
> temporary scene, then the initial proclamation of the gospel and the
> winning of converts does not conclude the missionary task. Forming
> believers into mature Christian congregations, providing theological
> and pastoral counsel against the dangers arising from inside and
> outside churches, strengthening believers both individually and
> corporately as they face suffering and persecution, so that they will

stand fast in the Lord, all fall within the scope of what is involved in continuing the mission of the exalted Lord Jesus Christ.[1]

Paul viewed his work as an organic whole. When he wrote to Timothy about God's mission purpose, he added an interesting comment about his own ministry:

> And for this purpose I was appointed a herald and an apostle . . . and a true and faithful teacher of the Gentiles. (1 Tim. 2: 7)

He uses three phrases which might represent the three successive stages of missionary work:

- Herald—someone who declares the message, the evangelist
- Apostle—the church planter
- Teacher—the one who encourages growth in discipleship

It makes sense, of course, for there is an obvious continuity from evangelism to church planting to growth and maturity. We should not create a division between evangelism and discipleship, or justification and sanctification, or conversion and Christian maturity. There ought to be a single integrated process from coming to faith in Christ to growing into mature Christlikeness.

So we are right to ask: what should be the ultimate outcome of such mission? What might such maturity look like? And what is the source of the nourishment and growth which Paul longs to see as he writes to the Colossian believers? Paul provides the answer:

> So then, just as you received Christ Jesus as Lord, continue to live your lives in him, rooted and built up in him, strengthened in the faith as you were taught, and overflowing with thankfulness. (Col. 2: 6, 7)

---

1. Andreas J. Köstenberger & Peter T. O'Brien, *Salvation to the Ends of the Earth: A biblical theology of mission*, New Studies in Biblical Theology (Leicester: Apollos, 2001), p. 268.

Some years ago, Bible teacher Dick Lucas highlighted three themes from these core verses. He expressed it like this:

> *As you received Christ Jesus as Lord, so live in him*
> *As you were rooted, be built up*
> *As you were taught, be strengthened in the faith.*

These represent three themes which describe the kind of growth that God longs for.

1. Christlikeness:
As you received Christ Jesus as Lord, so live in him.

The important connection is seen in verse 6. First, you have 'received Christ'. This means receiving or taking in the truth of the gospel. The Colossians had received what Paul had taught about Christ, his death and resurrection, and they had accepted that gospel message. Paul writes in the same way to the Corinthians:

> . . . I want to remind you of the gospel I preached to you, which you
> received and on which you have taken your stand. By this gospel you
> were saved, if you hold firmly to the word I have preached to you.
> (1 Cor. 15: 1, 2)

Receiving Christ

So they had 'received' the word of the gospel. But further, they had exercised faith not just in the teaching, but in Jesus himself. They had *received him*. This was the beginning of their new life in Christ, the start of their Christian discipleship. That's why in Colossians 2: 6, Paul says we have received 'Christ Jesus as Lord'. This means that, in turning to Christ, I acknowledge his right to rule every area of my life. And that leads to the second part of our phrase: as you received Christ Jesus as Lord, *so live in him.*

We know why this connection is so important. It's impossible for a disciple of Jesus to say, 'I've received Christ as Lord' and then fail to live a life that is dependent on him and obedient to him. Paul is implying: you have begun your discipleship by committing yourself to Jesus Christ as Lord. Now make good that profession, and shape your life by living under his Lordship.

Taking the shape of Christ

To underline the point, Paul uses an interesting expression when writing to the Galatians: 'until Christ is formed in you' (Gal. 4: 19). As John Stott comments, 'He is not satisfied that Christ *dwells* in them; he longs to see Christ *formed* in them, to see them transformed into the image of Christ, "until you take the shape of Christ" (NEB)'.[2]

So here is the first challenge to maturity: it is a call to live in Christ and to be like Christ. It is the call to godly living. It is for this reason that, in his first letter, John makes the point so directly:

> Whoever claims to live in him must live as Jesus did. (1 Jn. 2: 6)

The word translated 'mature' in the New Testament is sometimes translated 'perfect' or 'complete', and we find it in the letter of James. He is longing that Christian disciples would be 'mature and complete, lacking nothing' (Jas. 1: 4). James urges us to live in an integrated way. He is concerned with integrity, with bringing all of life together under the Lordship of Christ. He wants to see every part of the Christian life, and every aspect of Christian community, demonstrating the reality of Christian faith.

Living like Christ

Perhaps you have watched a TV news report where the sound and vision are 'out of sync'. We try to match what is being said with the animated face on the screen, but it's almost impossible. It's hard to take it seriously. In the

---

2. John Stott, *The Message of Galatians* (Leicester: IVP, 2021), p. 116.

same way, when a Christian's life fails to match up with their words, we give up listening. This kind of inconsistency destroys credibility, and we can't take them seriously. But where a Christian lives their words, keeps their promises and embodies the truth, then Christian community is built up and Christian mission is enhanced. This one quality can transform the life of our churches and make our Christian witness credible.

> Where a Christian lives their words, keeps their promises and embodies the truth, then Christian community is built up and Christian mission is enhanced

We know that this is a challenge all around the world. It has bubbled up in the context of our Langham seminars for pastors and preachers. In Hong Kong, I was told that Chinese pastors preach well, but can behave terribly at home. In Africa, most countries appeal that any training event for pastors must include a session on being a godly husband and acting faithfully in marriage and family life. (More positively, I was encouraged to receive an email from a woman in Indonesia, whose husband was part of the training programme. She wrote, 'I would like to know more about Langham Preaching, because not only does my husband preach better, he is a much nicer person'!)

We know this is a huge challenge for churches everywhere. Missiologist David Smith has written about Rwanda, and he explained that Christians 'in all denominational traditions found themselves asking how it could be that a region of Africa noted for its evangelization and often lauded as an example of continuous revival provided the cultural and ethnic context for a holocaust of unimaginable barbarity and wickedness . . . A distressed Catholic bishop observed: "the Christian message is not being heard. After a century of evangelization we have to begin again because the best catechists were the first to go out with machetes in their hands".'[3]

---

3. David Smith, *Against the Stream: Christianity and Mission in an Age of Globalization* (Leicester: IVP, 2003), p. 57.

The disastrous decline of churches in the western world is the result of multiple factors, but surely it is in no small part due to inconsistency—a failure to live like Christ. Whether it is the moral failure of church leaders, the ugly in-fighting within congregations, the failure to live distinct and attractive Christian lives, the inability to articulate the life-giving truth of the gospel beyond the walls of our ghetto—all these things betray the fact that we have failed to live under Christ's Lordship.

Our task, then, is to ensure our church is making the connection—having received Christ Jesus as Lord, we are to live in him. This will be reflected in our focussed attention on discipleship, whether amongst children and youth, families, young professionals, leaders and the elderly. The need for such growth is filled out still further in Colossians 2: 6, 7 with a second exhortation.

> The imagery of being rooted not only implies that I have a constant source of life for my spiritual growth, but it also means I am totally secure

2. Spiritual growth:
As you were rooted . . . be built up.

Once again, there are two inter-connected realities in the life of the Christian believer. First, you were rooted—the tense of the verb means that this is something that has happened in the life of the believer once and for all. You are inextricably united with Christ himself. You are settled. The imagery of being rooted not only implies that I have a constant source of life for my spiritual growth, but it also means I am totally secure—I can't be uprooted. 'No one will snatch them out of my hand', Jesus insisted (Jn. 10: 28). '[Nothing] will be able to separate us from the love of God', Paul affirmed (Rom. 8: 39). I am securely rooted.

But there is no room for complacency. Now, mixing his metaphors, Paul urges the believer to be built up, brick by brick. This is a challenge to continuous spiritual growth. It is vital for each Christian, but it is also essential for the sustainability of local churches.

Sustainable growth

When she was at school, one of my daughters was offered some stick insects by a friend. In fact, she was offered something like sixty of them. Her friend held on to a similar number, but wanted Becky to take the others. She thought about it carefully, but finally decided that, if she had that number, there were sure to be many casualties. So she took ten insects: she would rather care properly for a smaller number than face the trauma of multiple bereavements!

You sense a similar concern amongst the apostles. As we have stressed, they too were concerned that their mission was sustainable, that young churches should be nurtured and grow to maturity. In the book of Acts, we see that they deliberately returned to encourage the churches 'to be built up', to keep on growing, in numbers but also in maturity.

> Then they returned to Lystra, Iconium and Antioch, strengthening the disciples and encouraging them to remain true to the faith. (Acts 14: 21, 22)

Continuous growth

The Greek word for disciple (literally, 'learner') was a favourite term in Luke's writing, demonstrating that every believer must continually grow. It was deliberate apostolic strategy to return to the young Christian communities, to encourage them forward, and to provide practical teaching and structural support to ensure that this happened.

The Latin American theologian, René Padilla, has written about various contemporary missionary challenges, the first of which is the challenge of discipleship. After commenting on the extraordinary growth of the church in Africa and Latin America, he observes: 'This fantastic numerical growth, however, has its dangers. One of them, perhaps the most obvious one, is superficiality.'[4]

A few years ago, I participated in a consultation for those involved in Christian ministry in central Asia. It was heartening to see the steady growth of mission across some very demanding territories. But several of us noted an imbalance: there were large numbers of church planters, bravely committed to establishing new Christian communities, but among the several hundred people present, there were very few who represented the vital ministries of pastors and teachers, who would be nurturing young believers and encouraging mature congregational growth. As we read the accounts in Acts, the apostles demonstrate a sustained commitment to strengthening the disciples, congregation by congregation, and this doubtless reflected a close engagement with them in teaching, warning, reminding, loving, and encouraging.

This was Paul's big concern: that the church should have pastor-teachers 'to equip his people for works of service, so that the body of Christ may be built up until we all reach unity in the faith and in the knowledge of the Son of God and become mature, attaining to the whole measure of the fullness of Christ.' (Eph. 4: 12, 13)

First, then, having received Christ, we are to live in him: that's the call to Christlikeness. Second, having been rooted, we are to be built up: that's the call to spiritual growth. And undergirding these commitments lies a third theme.

3. Christian understanding:
As you were taught, be strengthened in the faith.

This third aspect of growth is a call to deepen our Christian understanding. Paul expresses it in verse 7 of Colossians 2, variously translated as 'strengthened in the faith as you were taught' (NIV), 'established in the faith as you

---

4. C. René Padilla, *Mission Between the Times* (Carlisle: Langham Monographs, 2010), p. 21.

were taught' (ESV), 'becoming more and more sure of the faith as you were taught it' (Phillips).

Paul places great stress on understanding. Don't just hold to the faith you were taught, he urges us; you are to increase in your knowledge of the truth and in your experience of its power. This is just as Peter encourages us: we are to 'grow in grace and in the knowledge of our Lord and Saviour Jesus Christ' (2 Pet. 3: 18). Growth in Christian understanding is one of the most significant marks of a healthy church.

> Growth in Christian understanding is one of the most significant marks of a healthy church

Our biggest crisis

Here we face another challenge, and one with global dimensions. In his opening address as the newly appointed Secretary-General of the World Evangelical Alliance, Thomas Schirrmacher spoke of the biggest crisis facing the evangelical church around the world. What do you think that might be? We could suggest religious persecution, or the growing threat of Islam, or the rise of secularism. But according to Schirrmacher, 'the biggest crisis is the growing lack of biblical literacy worldwide.' He continued, 'beyond all theological differences, financial problems, and political questions our biggest problem is that Bible knowledge is fading away.'

In an interesting book focussed on this aspect of healthy church growth, Jim Packer and Gary Parrett appealed for a contemporary form of catechesis for churches. They define catechesis as 'the church's ministry of grounding and growing God's people in the gospel and its implications for doctrine, direction, duty and delight'.[5] In commenting about church growth, they observe the significance of heightened evangelistic efforts, 'but in practice

---

5. J. I. Packer & Gary Parrett, *Grounded in the Gospel* (Baker Books, 2010), p. 182. Further quotation from p. 72.

this has often meant that while we are concerned that people *come* to church, we have not thought deeply enough about what they will *become* in time within the church.' So they propose a renewed commitment to growth in understanding, and provide helpful guidance of what must be taught and how that is best done.

Many of the New Testament letters express concern about immaturity, and call individuals and communities to grow up. Paul's critique of the Corinthians is one obvious example.

> Brothers, I do not address you as spiritual, but as worldly—mere infants in Christ. I gave you milk, not solid food, for you were not ready for it. Indeed, you are still not ready. You are still worldly. For since there is jealousy and quarrelling among you, are you not worldly? Are you not acting like mere human beings? (1 Cor. 3: 1–3)

It is this which lies behind Paul's concern in Colossians 2. *As you were taught, be established in the truth.* Growth in understanding is a vital strategy in church growth.

Think for a moment about Paul's commitment to the church in Ephesus. He stayed in the city for at least two years, and the account in Acts 19 reminds us of his various strategies both to evangelize and to teach. Luke records that Paul taught daily in the lecture hall of Tyrannus, which could well have represented some five hours a day of teaching. In his book about Christian maturity[6], Sinclair Ferguson calculated that this represented the equivalent of fifty years of three 40-minute sermons a week—all packed into his relatively brief stay in the city. Paul expected a level of maturity in his fellow believers that would be a challenge for us in the twenty-first century.

Teaching one another

Growing healthy churches means creating an appetite for truth. We are to be constant learners, growing in our understanding, experiencing the power

---

6. Sinclair B. Ferguson, *Maturity: Growing Up and Going On in the Christian Life* (Edinburgh: Banner of Truth, 2019), pp. 16, 17.

of God's word, and demonstrating its authenticity in our lives. Just like the Colossians believers, we too face the threat of false teachers. Whether it be the prosperity gospel, or powerful church leaders who hang loose to Bible teaching, or churches in the West impacted by liberal theology, or churches which marginalise the teaching of God's word, growth in understanding must be a priority for the protection, health and wellbeing of congregations large and small.

The good news is that, across many parts of the majority world, there are wonderful signs of growth in understanding, in formal and informal training, and in committed Bible teachers who are strengthening the church.

Some years ago, I visited northern India, having been invited to participate in a training event for a church-planting ministry in Uttar Pradesh. There were some 1,000 church planters present, representing a small army of younger leaders, working to establish churches across the State. We gathered under a large marquee for a full week, studying the book of Acts together. I discovered that this was their regular discipline: for one full week every month, they gathered together to work on Bible books. It was an extraordinary investment of time and energy, and a significant logistical and financial challenge.

Why such a big investment? The leaders replied that it was because the majority of the church planters had been converted from a Hindu background. So now they needed to build an entirely new worldview, a biblical worldview. For this reason they worked month by month on understanding the Bible's story line, grasping the content of Bible books, learning the core biblical themes and doctrines. And this was not for their sake alone, but so that in turn they could teach and train the churches which they were planting.

I couldn't help contrast this with the trend in my own country. Not long ago there was an article in a national newspaper which reported that church sermons were getting shorter and shorter—I think approaching an average 12 minutes. Doubtless with a wry smile, the journalist then added: 'This is a remarkable tribute to the power of intercessory prayer.' But this trend is troubling. Our churches are facing ever greater challenges, and have an urgent need for understanding and applying the truth of Scripture. How much we need to 'let the word of Christ dwell in you richly, teaching and admonishing one another in all wisdom', as Paul urges us in Colossians 3: 16 (ESV). We will address this theme more fully in chapter 4.

Here then are the foundations for growing healthy churches. The purpose is that Christian believers and local churches grow up into Christ, discovering their maturity in Him. That will be evidenced by these three essential qualities: Christlikeness, spiritual growth, and Christian understanding. Growing healthy churches begins by encouraging growth in Christ. This must be our fundamental congregational goal.

> . . . if you continue in your faith, established and firm, not moved from the hope held out in the gospel.' (Col. 1: 23)

> He is the one we proclaim, admonishing and teaching everyone with all wisdom, so that we may present everyone fully mature in Christ.' (Col. 1: 28)

> . . . just as you received Christ Jesus as Lord, continue to live your lives in him, rooted and built up in him, strengthened in the faith as you were taught, and overflowing with thankfulness. (Col. 2: 6, 7)

DISCUSSION AND APPLICATION

1. *Leaders who are biblically literate*
    It is clear that Paul gave everything he had to the task of bringing
    believers to maturity. We can see his energetic commitment as he
    describes his priorities: 'To this end I strenuously contend with all the
    energy Christ so powerfully works in me.' (Col. 1: 29)

    *   To what extent are our leaders growing in maturity themselves?
        How can we encourage this?

    *   What is needed to train the next generation of leaders who will
        demonstrate the qualities of growth which we have looked at in
        Colossians 2: 6, 7?

2. *Church priorities and programmes*
    In the book referred to by Packer and Parrett, it is suggested that
    churches have become preoccupied by other priorities, and are in
    danger of neglecting a carefully constructed and executed teaching
    programme.

    *   Is that true and, if so, what we can do about it?

    *   How can we shape teaching and training programmes at
        different levels of need and understanding?

    *   How are we strengthening the preaching and teaching ministry,
        which is so central to healthy growth to maturity? (We develop
        this more fully in chapter 4.)

    Whatever level of ability our congregation has in reading Scripture, we
    should encourage such disciplines as memorizing, discussing, praying,
    and applying.

    *   What can be done to help congregations engage with the truth
        through active listening?

    *   How can we provide help for home group leaders, and others
        who have a ministry of the word—youth leaders, women's
        workers, evangelists, church planters, pastoral workers?

3.   *One-to-one support*

> 'Let the word of Christ dwell in you richly, teaching and
> admonishing one another with all wisdom . . .' (Col. 3: 16).

The preacher and author John Stott often spoke about how he had
been helped in his growth in Christ through the intentional friendship of
others. This is what he wrote in his commentary on 2 Timothy:

> 'I thank God for the man who led me to Christ and for the
> extraordinary devotion with which he nurtured me in the early
> years of my Christian life. He wrote to me every week for, I
> think, seven years. He also prayed for me every day. I believe
> he still does. I can only begin to guess what I owe, under God,
> to such a faithful friend and pastor.'[7]

- How can we be more intentional in establishing a one-to-one
  ministry which encourages fellow believers?

4.   *Family responsibility*

> 'These commandments that I give you today are to be on your
> hearts. Impress them on your children. Talk about them when
> you sit at home and when you walk along the road, when you
> lie down and when you get up. Tie them as symbols on your
> hands and bind them on your foreheads. Write them on the
> doorframes of your houses and on your gates.' (Dt. 6: 6–9)

Deuteronomy 6 reminds us of the responsibility to teach the family.

- In what ways can we help families to teach, train and nurture
  their children and young people?

- How can we ensure that parents see their first responsibility as
  nurturing spiritual life and growth in their children?

- What resources might they need, and how can we provide these?

(Here are some background passages: Deuteronomy 6: 4–9; Psalm
78: 1–8; Ephesians 6: 4; 2 Timothy 1: 5.)

---

7. John Stott, *The Message of 2 Timothy: Guard the Gospel,* Bible Speaks Today (Leicester:
IVP, 1984), p. 29.

5.   *Personal growth*

   •   In what ways can personal devotion, biblical understanding, and
       obedient discipleship be nurtured in the life of each believer in
       our church?

Sometimes it doesn't happen because of very high expectations of
what should be done, and in busy lives, or with a busy family, it all looks
impossible.

   •   Even if only with small changes, in what ways can we help
       believers take steps forward?

CHAPTER 2

Growth in holiness

Base passage: 1 Thessalonians

L et's suppose that you are playing a game of word association with a group of friends. You are each given a postcard and are invited to write down words that surface in your mind when the leader says the word, 'holiness'.

What would you write down? Here is an intriguing list provided by John White some years ago. Maybe you can identify with some of the associations he makes:

> Thinness; hollow-eyed gauntness; beards; sandals; long robes; stone cells; no sex; no jokes; hair shirts; frequent cold baths; fasting; hours of prayer; wild rocky deserts; getting up at 4.00 am; clean fingernails; stained glass; self-humiliation.[1]

What do you think? It is strangely religious, isn't it? And, sadly, that's what the word *holy* has come to mean. It's associated with painful and rigorous effort, with withdrawal from normal life, with the world of the weird and wacky religious fanatic. And this is one reason why we discuss the subject of holiness less and less. It's not on our agenda these days. David Wilkinson once pointed out that if you advertise a talk on the Christian view of sex, or healing in the power of the Spirit, you can guarantee an excited, packed congregation. But a talk on holiness may be greeted with the same enthusiasm as a lecture on advanced tax returns. Holiness gets a bad press. When a British publisher brought out a new edition of the Bible they simply called

---

1. John White, *The Fight* (Leicester: IVP, 1997), p. 179.

it 'The Bible'. In response to concerned questions, a spokesman said, 'we dropped the word "Holy" to give it a more mass market appeal.'

The truth of the matter is that holiness is not to be locked away as a religious word of limited relevance to our lives. Holiness is to shape who we are. It should describe everything about us—our identity, our attitude, our behaviour, and our corporate life as God's distinct people. It has to do with the everyday, with the mundane of our lives and relationships, such that it removes any distinction between the so-called 'sacred' and the so-called 'secular'. It is to describe who we are and what we are to become.

In his book based on some of the apostle Paul's prayers, Don Carson mentions that a study by the Princeton Religion Research Centre demonstrated that, alongside some increase in church attendance over recent years, there was a marked decline in professing Christians who thought there was any connection between Christianity and morality. He wrote: 'Much of American Christianity is returning to raw paganism: the ordinary pagan can be ever so religious without any necessary entailment in ethics, morality, self-sacrifice or integrity.'[2] Surveys find little difference when comparing the behaviour of born-again Christians before and after their conversion experience. While statistics might be more readily available in US, we can presume that the situation is very similar in other countries.

Godliness and mission

As we read the New Testament, we see that there is a close connection between holiness and mission. The early Christians couldn't afford any inconsistency. They were being watched. Their lives, their work, their families, their values, their response under pressure—all of these had to support their radical message in the first century.

> There is a close connection between holiness and mission

---

2. D. A. Carson, *A Call to Spiritual Reformation* (Leicester: IVP, 1992), p. 14.

Paul's first letter to the Thessalonians describes the kind of church growth that really matters. It is one of the letters which has most to say about godliness and Christian service. It describes a life that is pleasing to God, and the theme is prominent in every chapter.

> You know how we lived among you for your sake. (1: 5)

> You are witnesses . . . of how holy, righteous and blameless we were among you . . . (2: 10)

> May he strengthen your hearts so that you will be blameless and holy in the presence of our God and Father when our Lord Jesus comes with all his holy ones. (3: 13)

> As for other matters . . . we instructed you how to live in order to please God . . . (4: 1)

> It is God's will that you should be sanctified . . . (4: 3)

> For God did not call us to be impure, but to live a holy life. (4: 7)

> . . . always strive to do what is good . . . (5: 15)

> May God himself . . . sanctify you through and through. (5: 23)

In this chapter we will look at this aspect of church growth, and will examine the two prayers or benedictions which focus on this theme, as well as some of Paul's writing regarding his own leadership. But first, we should remember what the church at Thessalonica was like, since it is probably similar to many of the churches known to us.

i) It was a young church

Paul was with these believers for just three weeks. The church was predominantly a Gentile church, made up of young Christians, with young leaders, living in a hostile situation. What chance would such a church have of being planted, let alone maturing? They were among the first Christians in all of Europe—and what was their hope of survival? Given the pressures which this little Christian community was under, how could it possibly remain steady?

In 1 Thessalonians 3, Paul expresses his concern, and indicated that he couldn't wait any longer for news: he sent Timothy to find out how they were doing. So it was a huge relief to receive Timothy's encouraging report: 'For now we really live, since you are standing firm in the Lord.' (1 Thess. 3: 8)

The letter is very relevant to the contemporary church around the world. In situations of persecution or opposition, the same question arises: can the church stand firm against wind and tide? How can the church in northern Nigeria keep the faith? How can the small minority of 4,000 evangelicals in Turkey cope with the opposition? How can the churches in the various Islamic Republics stand firm? How can small assemblies with limited resources manage to sustain their work and witness?

These are specially urgent questions given that so many churches face growing pressures—the temptations of living in a secular society, the pressures of standing up for Jesus in a plural context where he is denied, the challenge of opposition. And this leads to the second characteristic of this Christian community.

ii) It was a persecuted church

There are two ways in which the passage describes how these pressures manifested themselves.

First, *they were distracted by trials.* Paul says in 1 Thessalonians 3: 3 that he sent Timothy to strengthen and encourage them, 'so that no one would be unsettled by these trials.' The pressures facing these young Christians could really shake their faith. The word is used in the New Testament for trials, persecution, suffering, and trouble of all kinds. It was not so much the fact of trials, but the *intensity* of these trials that so concerned Paul.

Second, *they were disturbed by Satan.* 'I was afraid that in some way the tempter might have tempted you and our labours might have been in vain.' (1 Thess. 3: 5) We see the same at the end of chapter 2: 'we wanted to come and see you—certainly I, Paul, did, again and again—but Satan blocked our way.' (1 Thess. 2: 18) Satan is spoken of in every part of the New Testament, whether in the account of Jesus' own temptations or the temptation of his disciples, or in relation to his disruptive influence, causing division in churches, or hindering the work of missionaries like Paul. But the interesting thing to notice is how Paul talks about these pressures:

> You know quite well that we were destined for them. In fact, when
> we were with you, we kept telling you that we would be persecuted.
> And it turned out that way, as you well know. (1 Thess. 3: 3, 4)

Calvin commented that it was almost as if God had told them that they were Christians on this condition—you *will* suffer. But the verse implies something more. The suffering that they endured was not just a matter of chance or blind fate: verse 3 implies that this is something within God's purpose. You are 'destined' or 'appointed' for these trials. Since we know that the Lord is sovereign, we also know that, whatever the circumstances that our church is facing, the situation is not out of control. The Lord will keep his church. He will remain faithful.

iii) It was a model church

We also notice that the opening words of Paul's letter commend them as an example of Christian growth: 'You became a model to all the believers in Macedonia and Achaia.' (1: 7) This encouragement is set in the middle of a sequence of phrases in chapter 1. It is a chain reaction:

> v. 5   the gospel came to you
> v. 6   you welcomed the message
> v. 8   it rang out from you everywhere.

And the same ripple effect is described in terms of modelling and emulating. It was not simply proclaiming a message which they had received. It was also a manner of life which became a compelling example to others:

> v. 6   you became imitators of us
> v. 7   you became a model to all the believers in Macedonia.

From the seaport of Thessalonica, the message rippled out, echoing around the mountain villages, spreading far and wide. And it was not just a message, but a model. People heard about the impact of the gospel on the church. It had a ripple effect not only on surrounding cities and provinces, but it crossed time and generations, as verse 8 suggests: '. . . your faith in God has become known everywhere.'

Despite extraordinary pressure, they were standing firm, full of faith and love: 'For now we really live, since you are standing firm in the Lord.' (3: 8) Paul was so thankful for this encouraging news that it clearly energized him. They were *standing firm,* a word which includes the idea of stability, firmness and steadfastness. They were rock solid! And we should note Paul's qualifying language: 'standing firm *in the Lord.*' These Thessalonian believers were able to sustain their steadfast commitment by being in close union with the Lord, as we emphasised in the last chapter. He was the rock on which they stood, the one who strengthened their communal resolve to live with faith and love.

But as we would expect, Paul made it clear that there was room for yet more growth. It was a work in progress. He wanted to visit to 'supply what is lacking in your faith' (3: 10), an expression used by Mark for fishermen mending holes in their nets. There was still plenty to be done. And so for this reason, as we shall see, Paul was also committed to pray for them. We should not miss the fact that such prayer is a fundamental aspect of how a healthy church can be sustained.

To learn more about growth in godliness we will now turn to three sections of the letter. The first and the last relate to the two prayers which help shape the structure of the letter. They are two benedictions. One is the prayer of chapter 3: 11–13, which both brings the first section of the letter to a close and anticipates some of the themes of the second section. Then there is the second benediction, found in chapter 5: 23–28, which brings the letter to a close.

> Prayer is a fundamental aspect of how a healthy church can be sustained

We turn first to the prayer found in chapter 3.

1. The church's calling: *1 Thessalonians 3: 11–4: 8*

Paul is a great example of how to care for a local church. One of the key ways in which he expressed his affectionate care for them is that he prayed for them. We find this in all of his letters. We notice here that it is committed prayer: 'night and day we pray most earnestly . . .' (3: 10) He has already said that he works 'night and day' so as not to be a burden to them (2: 9). So how are we to understand this expression?

I wonder if you have had this experience. Maybe a close friend or relative is having a serious operation; or your child is in the middle of an important exam or a job interview. You know the feeling: you can hardly wait for news of how it has gone. But, as you wait, every few minutes it surfaces in your mind again, and you pray for them. A while ago, my neighbour was seriously ill with cancer and, in his final days, he was on my mind and in my prayers quite frequently. We do this because we are so concerned about the situation, so concerned about their welfare that it naturally springs to mind, maybe every few minutes in the midst of many other things. That's exactly how it should be as we pray for one another in the church. Fellow Christians under pressure need us to bring their situation to God. And so it was that Paul felt that responsibility for the hard-pressed believers to whom he was writing.

Depending on God

As we reflect on growing healthy churches, we discover an encouraging truth which explains why we need this kind of prayerful dependence: it is ultimately God's work. We can see this explained in the passage in several ways.

First, Paul's ministry was dependent on God's providential oversight:

> Now may our God and Father himself and our Lord Jesus clear the
> way for us to come to you. (3: 11)

29

And sure enough, God answered. Paul was eventually able to visit them again at least twice (compare Acts 20: 2 & 3). We know that Satan's purpose is to hinder the work, but ultimately God's purposes for his church are unstoppable.

Second, our spiritual growth is in God's hands.

> May the Lord make your love increase and overflow for each other
> and for everyone else, just as ours does for you. (3: 12)

And this is a significant partnership. On the one hand, Paul sees it as God's work: 'the Lord make your love increase . . .' (3: 12) But then, in the next chapter, he underlines their responsibility to act: 'you do love all the brothers . . . Yet we urge you . . . to do so more and more . . .' (4: 10) There is a God-centredness about his appeals, but we can see that this stimulates our sense of responsibility rather than lessening it. In Christian living, we co-operate with God to activate his purposes in our lives.

Third, we come to the prayer for holiness, where again it is clear that this is something which God will achieve:

> May he strengthen your hearts so that you will be blameless and holy
> in the presence of our God and Father when our Lord Jesus comes
> with all his holy ones. (3: 13)

'Blameless' means that, on that future day when Jesus returns, nothing will stand against us; none of Satan's accusations will harm us.

Anticipating Christ's return

As we find throughout this letter, the expectation of Christ's future return is a key stimulus for us here and now. There is no greater encouragement to live the life of faith and love and hope—to live in holiness and to stand firm—than the prospect of Christ's return.

> On that future day when Jesus returns, nothing will stand against us; none of Satan's accusations will harm us

This often becomes more significant as we grow older. Fixing our eyes on Jesus, the coming King, sets all of our trials and Satanic pressures in perspective. It is the motivation to live holy lives. John expresses that same truth: 'But we know that when Christ appears, we shall be like him, for we shall see him as he is. All who have this hope in him purify themselves, just as he is pure.' (1 Jn. 3: 2, 3)

> There is no greater encouragement to live the life of faith and love and hope—to live in holiness and to stand firm—than the prospect of Christ's return

On the foundation of such a prayer, we come to Paul's practical teaching. It is an encouragement 'to live in order to please God' (1 Thess. 4: 1), and we notice that Paul makes the point repeatedly:

> It is God's will that you should be sanctified . . . (4: 3)

> For God did not call us to be impure, but to live a holy life. (4: 7)

Paul makes clear that his teaching has the authority of Christ (4: 2), and he now outlines what this kind of godly living in the church should look like.

> . . . that you should avoid sexual immorality; that each of you should learn to control your own body in a way that is holy and honourable, not in passionate lust like the pagans, who do not know God; and that in this matter no one should wrong or take advantage of a brother or sister. (4: 3–6)

As we have already seen (3: 13), we shall be holy on that day when we see Christ. But now Paul uses a related word that refers to the process of being made holy, rather than the state of holiness: 'it is God's will that you should be sanctified . . .' (4: 3)

What is the process? It is a commitment to bring our practice into line with our Christian calling and our status as belonging to God's family, a point made clearly in the next verse: 'For God did not call us to be impure, but to live a holy life.' (4: 7)

Growth which pleases God

These are demanding verses that deserve our study and prayerful reflection. They represent a call to a lifetime of Christian growth. It is the kind of growth that is fundamental to God's will for his people; it is growth which truly pleases God; and it is growth which is empowered by God, who gives us his Holy Spirit (4: 3–8).

I am sure that every reader is aware that today we can no longer assume in our local churches that there is a common understanding of sexual ethics and behaviour. We live in a context of confusion amongst believers; most of us are in societies where there is not only uncertainty in the church, but increasingly hostile opposition in society to the biblical norms of sexuality.

This raises inevitable questions for us as we reflect on growing healthy churches. It is vital that this aspect of our calling—the call to holy living—is prioritised in our teaching and training, our pastoral ministry, in our mutual accountability, and also in our supportive prayers for our churches, just as it was for Paul.

We have seen that, while we are called to take responsibility to grow in godliness, there is no way we can do this unaided. We know that, as we turn to him, the Lord will equip us and prepare us for that future day when we will stand in his presence:

> May he strengthen your hearts so that you will be blameless and holy
> in the presence of our God and Father when our Lord Jesus comes
> with all his holy ones. (3: 13)

2. The church's leadership: *1 Thessalonians 1: 5; 2: 10*

We have seen that 1 Thessalonians is full of encouragement to our churches to grow in holiness. In the process of teaching this, the letter also has something significant to say to leaders. It has been well said that the spiritual health of leaders largely determines the spiritual health of those they lead, not least because of the powerful effect of godly example.

I write these words in the wake of recent news that several prominent Christian leaders have fallen into sin, and there has been a great deal on social media about the ripple effects of such failure. One blogger has written: 'It seems that hardly a month goes by without another scandal from a 'Celebrity Pastor'. Abuse of power, sexual sin, financial irregularities, cover-ups—each one a crushing blow; another straw heaped on the back of an already-straining camel, namely the public credibility of Christianity.'[3]

> The spiritual health of leaders largely determines the spiritual health of those they lead

All of us know that growth in holiness is vital for every leader, first for their own wellbeing, then for the wellbeing of those for whom they care, then for the wellbeing of Christian witness—but most of all, because this is the will of God, as we have already seen.

Consistent living

In his book *Leadership Jazz*, Max De Pree describes the birth of his granddaughter, Zoe. She was born prematurely and weighed just over half a kilo; she was so small that his wedding ring could slide up her arm all the way to her shoulder. The doctor who first examined her told him that she had a 5 to 10 per cent chance of living. To complicate matters, Zoe's biological father had left the marriage before Zoe was born. So a nurse explained to Max that, for the next several months, he should be the surrogate father. He should come to the hospital every day to visit Zoe, and he should stroke her with the tip of his finger, telling her how much he loved her, because 'she has to be able to connect your voice to your touch.' And Max De Pree

---

3. Liam Thatcher, 'Tracing the ripples from fallen pastors,' accessed on February 11, 2022, https://liamthatcher.com/2020/12/17/tracing-the-ripples-from-fallen-pastors/

comments: 'At the core of becoming a leader is the need always to connect one's voice and one's touch.'[4]

Godly leadership means that there is a clear correspondence between our words and our lives. Paul was also acutely aware of the importance of such consistency of life. When he spoke to the Ephesian elders, he stressed: 'Keep watch over yourselves and all of the flock of which the Holy Spirit has made you overseers.' (Acts 20: 28) He said the same to Timothy: 'Don't let anyone look down on you because you are young, but set an example to the believers in speech, in life, in love, in faith and in purity . . . Watch your life and your doctrine closely.' (1 Tim. 4: 12 & 16)

First priority

The order is significant in both exhortations: watch yourselves, watch your life, your godliness, your spiritual well-being, first. Indeed, Paul was fearful of the potential danger of helping others, but himself facing shipwreck (1 Cor. 9: 27), and so he engaged in demanding self-discipline in order to avoid being disqualified for the prize. There is therefore a seriousness about Paul's writing, not least because of the special temptations which leaders face.

Indeed, it seems that the New Testament writers were less concerned about the technical issues of how leaders were appointed, or what kind of leadership structures were to be adopted, or even what duties they were to perform. They were much more concerned about what kind of people they were to be.

In today's culture, Christian leaders will have an earned authority if their own lives are a strong moral example to others. Authority is not merely the result of strong pronouncements from the pulpit,

> Authority is not merely the result of strong pronouncements from the pulpit, but arises from the quality of life in day-to-day service

4. Max De Pree, *Leadership Jazz: The Essential Elements of a Great Leader*, (New York: Doubleday 1992[1] (Currency, 2008[2])), pp. 1–3.

but arises from the quality of life in day-to-day service. Paul demonstrates this in several ways.

a) The gospel must be embodied

First, let's look at the way in which Paul brought the gospel to the Thessalonians.

> . . . our gospel came to you not simply with words, but also with power, with the Holy Spirit and with deep conviction. You know how we lived among you for your sake. (1: 5)

Paul's expressions here demonstrate a vital combination of qualities which we too should display. The message was delivered in God's power and with conviction, and proclaimed in the Holy Spirit who empowered them and who pressed home the truth to the hearers. It was a combination of word and Spirit. But that was not all. There is a further phrase in verse 5 which, in the original text, is closely connected to the rest of the verse: our gospel came to you with power, *so 'you know how we lived among you for your sake.'* On several occasions Paul encourages the believers to 'remember how we lived'. The gospel was clearly bearing fruit in his own life, and it was this gospel combination that was so effective: God's word, proclaimed in the power of the Spirit, was demonstrated and embodied in the messenger himself.

This was exactly the burden of Jeremiah as he called the prophets of his day to be consistent in word and life. Not only had there been an appalling theological deterioration, but also a deep-set moral failure among the prophets. Instead of leading people away from sin, the prophets actually confirmed people in such activity: 'they live a lie', Jeremiah said.

A true prophet will be one whose own life is an embodiment of the truth. A prophet's life is part of his message. David Day once expressed it like this: 'He is not like a postman who can do what he likes in private as long as he goes on delivering letters.'[5]

---

5. David Day, *Jeremiah: Speaking for God in a Time of Crisis*, (Leicester: IVP, 1987), p. 89.

Phillips Brooks has written on the importance of preachers also living the life, and he illustrated it by the analogy of a train station employee who comes to believe that he has been to all the places he announces because of his long and loud heralding of them. And that's our danger: we teach it, we train others, but we fail to make the journey ourselves.

Authentic Christian ministry is when word, Spirit and life combine as they did in Paul. This is the kind of authority that really matters, and which carries the integrity and consistency for which people are searching.

> That's our danger: we teach it, we train others, but we fail to make the journey ourselves

b) Ministry must be modelled

We come next to a further ingredient of godly leadership. It is spelt out in 1 Thessalonians 2, and it is also seen in the way in which Paul carried out his leadership and pastoral ministry:

> You are witnesses, and so is God, of how holy, righteous and blameless we were among you who believed. For you know that we dealt with each of you as a father deals with his own children, encouraging, comforting and urging you to live lives worthy of God, who calls you into his kingdom and glory. (2: 10–12)

Godly example is an enormously influential ingredient in a healthy church. We often say that character is caught rather than taught. And it was clearly part of the apostolic strategy. Paul could say, 'Follow my example, as I follow the example of Christ.' (1 Cor. 11: 1) It was also why Paul was concerned to avoid the opposite effect: 'We put no stumbling block in anyone's path, so that our ministry will not be discredited. Rather, as servants of God we commend ourselves in every way . . .' (2 Cor. 6: 3, 4)

As a child I was involved in a small congregation in north London. At around ten years old, I encountered failure within the Christian community for the first time. It was discovered that the treasurer had been taking funds from the church over a period of years. In a small church like ours, the impact of this discovery was considerable. A prominent leader had been deceiving people. Someone whom we had seen as beyond failure had acted inconsistently. In many churches, such failure can paralyse the Christian community.

In fact, by God's grace, failure in our church was handled in a gracious and firm manner. The man was eventually restored and, with great humility, served the church in a number of quiet ways. I came to respect him enormously. As a very young believer, I learnt some important lessons: that we must pray for leaders, all of whom are vulnerable; that those who name the name of Christ must live his life; and that God can redeem failure.

In 1 Thessalonians 2, Paul is reinforcing the fact that there was nothing in his life which could be made an excuse for others not believing the Christian gospel or walking the pathway of Christian discipleship. His message and ministry were wedded to a godly life that made the gospel believable.

And not only that, he states in 1 Thessalonians 2: 11, 12 that this also shaped his pastoral ministry. Like a father he encouraged, comforted and urged those believers to 'live lives worthy of God . . .'

> His message and ministry were wedded to a godly life that made the gospel believable

The same is clear from the pastoral epistles, with their deliberate emphasis on the character profile of leaders. The leader must be 'above reproach' (1 Tim. 3: 2), displaying a rounded spiritual maturity that shapes the whole of life. As the Puritan Richard Sibbes wrote to Christian ministers, 'we must study as hard to live well as to preach well'.

The power of example

People learn best by being alongside such godly believers. The term 'mentoring' has become more familiar in church settings, but whatever term we use, this represents a vital part of Christian leadership. It means giving time to the shaping of other Christians through 'parental care'. The best leaders are those who model the Christian walk with integrity, whose vision and decision-making processes are shaped consistently by godly standards, and who display a Christlike attitude of gentleness and humility to those for whom they are responsible.

This is the leadership authority that is respected by a congregation, and leads to the appropriate emulation of leaders to which Scripture points (Phil. 4: 9; 1 Thess. 1: 5–7; Heb. 13: 7). As the American Puritan, Cotton Mather, expressed it:

> Examples do strangely charm us into imitation. When holiness is pressed upon us we are prone to think that it is a doctrine calculated for angels and spirits whose dwelling is not with flesh. But when we read the lives of them that excelled in holiness, though they were persons of like passions with ourselves, the conviction is wonderful and powerful.[6]

Part of that godly example will mean an ability to draw alongside those for whom God has given us responsibility. There is no hint in Paul's writing of a hierarchical leadership style, a professional indifference to the needs of those to whom he was speaking. Quite the reverse. There is probably no better description of pastoral ministry than his words in 1 Thessalonians 2:

> '. . . as apostles of Christ we could have asserted our authority. Instead, we were like young children among you. Just as a nursing mother cares for her children, so we cared for you. Because we loved you so much, we were delighted to share with you not only the gospel of God but also our lives as well.' (2: 6, 7)

Paul's leadership was expressed through an unreserved commitment to them. His ministry was wholehearted. He not only worked hard to support himself but he constantly gave himself to others. The metaphors that he uses convey a deep love for them, a motherly tenderness and gentleness.

---

6. Cotton Mather, in his *Ecclesiastical History of New England*.

Teaching and preaching are very demanding ministries, but they are not as demanding as sharing your life with those for whom you have leadership responsibility. Self-sacrifice lies at the heart of servant leadership, and this is simply following in the steps of the Lord Jesus himself (1 Peter 5: 1–4). Authenticity and authority in Christian leadership require that our lives embody our message, and that inevitably means a costly identification with those whom we are called to serve.

Paul's letter to the Thessalonians demonstrates how authoritative leadership is more spiritual and moral than it is technical and intellectual. It is founded on a sense of God's calling, shaped by a commitment to the authority of God's word, supported by the authority of godly example, and welcomed by the congregation because of its compassionate identification with them.

> Authenticity and authority in Christian leadership require that our lives embody our message, and that inevitably means a costly identification with those whom we are called to serve

3. The church's confidence: *1 Thessalonians 5: 23, 24*

As we reflect on growth in holiness, most of us will be acutely aware of our failure, both personal and corporate. It seems that the daily pull of sin, and the temptations of the world, the flesh and the devil, are constant.

In a wise book about Christian service, Paul Mallard expresses this accurately: 'The longer I live as a Christian, the more I hate the battle that no one else sees. It is the battle for holiness, the crusade against lust and greed and sloth and envy and anger and bitterness and pride . . . The greatest battle in Christian leadership is the battle for holiness.'[7]

---

7. Paul Mallard, *Staying Fresh* (Leicester: IVP, 2015), pp. 84, 85.

It is the fight of our lives. So how can we live up to our calling as individual believers and as a church?

It is especially encouraging to see that Paul closes his letter with strong assurances of the God who fulfils his promises, who keeps his word. The closing benediction is:

> May God himself, the God of peace, sanctify you through and through. May your whole spirit, soul and body be kept blameless at the coming of our Lord Jesus Christ. The one who calls you is faithful and he will do it. (5: 23, 24)

It is a hugely encouraging end to the letter. As we have seen, we are God's church, and God himself promises that he will complete the work he has begun. His purpose is to take sinners like us and restore the image, making us like his Son. He takes us as we are and he sets to work in making us what we should be. He restores us—and will restore all things—as he brings everything to completion in Jesus Christ.

He takes us as we are and he sets to work in making us what we should be

The other day I heard a true story about a former UK Member of Parliament called Enoch Powell. He was quite a distinctive character, with quite a distinctive appearance. One day, he was visiting a local village in his constituency, and happened to notice they were holding an Enoch Powell look-alike competition. So without saying anything, he entered the competition. He came third!

The Christian life is also about a look-alike programme, but one with guaranteed final perfection. The goal of growth in godliness is that we should look like Jesus. That has been God's restoration programme from the very beginning.

We notice three encouragements about Paul's closing prayer:

*First, it is **comprehensive**:*

> 'May your whole spirit, soul and body be kept blameless at the coming of our Lord Jesus Christ.' (1 Thess. 5: 23, 24)

The use of 'spirit, soul and body' is a way of saying that this is a complete transformation of the whole person. That is God's purpose, and that is what he will achieve in our lives. Growth in holiness means a radical commitment to live in Christ, to serve Christ, and to become like Christ.

The promise is clear: he will sanctify us completely. He will make us like himself. This is the culmination of the gospel story: we have been created in God's image, we have been marred by sin, but we will be finally and fully restored in the image of Christ. And this work is total and complete—body, soul, spirit.

*Second, it is **urgent**:*

> '. . . at the coming of our Lord Jesus Christ.' (5: 23)

The theme of Jesus' return is found at the end of every chapter in this letter. As we see at the end of chapter 4, the second coming of Christ is integral to our lives. It is the focus of our hope and the motivation for our service. And it's here too at the end of the letter. God is preparing us for that great event—'the coming of our Lord Jesus Christ.' Scripture urges us to get dressed, ready for that day. The night is almost over and the day is almost here, Paul told the Romans. 'So let us set aside the deeds of darkness and put on the armour of light . . . clothe yourselves with the Lord Jesus Christ . . .' (Rom. 13: 11–14)

We must keep our eyes on the horizon, and do so with a firm commitment to live for Christ here and now.

*Third, it is **guaranteed**:*

> 'The one who calls you is faithful, and he will do it.' (5: 24)

Paul closes his letter with the strong assurance from God himself, the one who keeps his word. He promises that he will complete the work he has begun. He will sanctify us fully. He will make us like Jesus.

Maybe some of our fellow believers in our local church wonder if they can keep it up. Perhaps there might be a young person who has just decided to follow Christ, but is uncertain about coping with the challenges of living for him. Or maybe there is an older person, fearful that in their final days of life they will lose their certainty or their assurance. For all of us, the promise holds good: 'The one who calls you is faithful, and he will do it.' God will finish what he began.

Paul had only been with the Thessalonian church for about three weeks, and, as he wrote to them, he longed that they should not only continue, but should find themselves faultless on the day when Jesus Christ returns. This small, young, persecuted community of believers had been urged to live godly lives, but had also been promised God's empowering provision and certain completion.

Christian discipleship is living between the times, because God has not yet finished what he began. The letter opened with this greeting: 'To the church of the Thessalonians in God the Father and in the Lord Jesus Christ.' (1: 1) And it ends with the encouraging reminder of the perfecting work of the Father and the sufficient grace of the Lord Jesus Christ: 'The grace of our Lord Jesus Christ be with you.' (5: 28)

DISCUSSION AND APPLICATION

1. *We should pray for this*
    It is impressive to see that the most obvious feature of Paul's concern
    for growing healthy churches is seen in his prayers for them. The
    New Testament letters highlight this frequently, and we have seen
    the prayers embedded in 1 Thessalonians that relate to the theme of
    holiness and godliness. He is praying for growth that pleases God.

    - To what extent is prayer a feature of our church life?
      Make a list of some of the key things that we should pray for
      in the local church—bearing in mind that 'our praying will be
      shaped by our profound desire to seek what is best for the
      people of God' (Don Carson).

    - How can we build such prayer into the daily and weekly life of
      our local church, or our training institutions?

    - How can we ensure that this kind of focussed prayer is fully part
      of our pastoral care within the church? How might such prayer
      become a normal part of pastoral encouragement and support?

2. *We should teach this*
    Over 30 years ago, John Stott commented on 1 Thessalonians and
    suggested that one of the great weaknesses of evangelical churches
    is our comparative neglect of Christian ethics, in both our teaching and
    our practice. 'In consequence, we have become known rather as people
    who preach the gospel than those who live and adorn it.'

    - Do you think this observation still applies to our churches? What
      more can be done to nurture growth in godliness such that the
      outside observer will see that the local church is a model of a
      morality and lifestyle shaped by the gospel?

    One danger we face is 'moralism', which suggests that, with a little
    more effort on our part and with the help of the Spirit, we will be able to
    live as we should.

    - Why does understanding gospel truth become essential if we are
      to live truly godly lives? How can we build the link in our teaching
      between the gospel of grace and the life of practical holiness?

- In our local church, how often do we teach the big themes of Christian living, as they relate to contemporary challenges—in areas such as marriage and the family, singleness, business ethics, human sexuality, pornography, corruption at work and in society? How can we help married couples whose relationship is under pressure, or people with same sex attraction, or people who struggle with singleness, or doctors with medical ethics, or workers with bosses who demand immoral behaviour?

- How can we help those teaching the Bible in our churches to be both faithful to Scripture and contemporary in their understanding of today's moral challenges, and therefore practical in their application of God's truth?

- Do we teach new believers right from the start that growth in godly living is at the heart of discipleship? How can we build this into our early teaching and training of young believers?

- How do we help parents to ensure that they are teaching their children God's good purposes for moral living? What resources could we provide for them?

3. *We should model this*

We have seen Paul's unashamed apologetic—he brought the gospel to them in word, in power, in full conviction, and all supported by a godly life. He could appeal to them as witnesses of his holy, righteous behaviour. He was a model to the believers, who in turn became a model to others. And this raises questions for us—for our leaders, our trainers, our parents, our youth workers.

- To what extent are our churches growing as a result of the godly lives which influence them? What more can be done to encourage our leaders in this area?

- All of us need the help and encouragement of other believers. What kind of accountability can be set in place to help leaders (at whatever level) to be faithful in their daily lives, feeling supported in their leadership work?

As Chuck Colson once said, 'The task of the church is not to make men and women happy; it is to make them holy'.

CHAPTER 3

Growth in unity[1]

Base passage: Ephesians 4: 1–6

A while ago, a friend of mine told me about her ordeal when she took her driving test. She was struggling to select the right gear at that critical moment, the hill-start. She fought with the gear stick, while the examiner, clipboard in hand, looked over his glasses wondering how long they would be there. 'Don't worry, love,' he said. 'They're all in the same box. All you've got to do is sort them out.'

It struck me that this piece of wisdom had a distinctly Pauline ring about it. The sentiment expresses the twin truths of the New Testament when it comes to the subject of Christian unity.

On the one hand, the Bible is absolutely clear about the unity of all true Christians: we belong to one Father, we are redeemed by one Lord Jesus Christ, and we are indwelt by one Holy Spirit. We're all in the same box. At the same time, the New Testament frequently focuses on the question of how that unity must be demonstrated, how the cogs and wheels must engage so that the Christian community can make progress.

Paul's exhortation is that we make every effort to maintain the unity of the Spirit. We know this is vital.

First, because of what is happening in our culture. Social commentators tell us that we now live in a world of walls. There are divisions everywhere.

---

1. I have elaborated this theme in my book, *Essentially One: stiving for the unity God love'* (IVP, 2020).

Apparently, there are at least 65 countries that have erected barriers along their borders, reflecting a wide variety of divisions and hostilities.[2]

It's not simply to do with fences and walls, but with a growing sense of social division, which manifests itself in tribalism of all kinds. This has been clear in relation to the polarised Brexit debate, in recent US elections, and in the debates about COVID vaccines and climate change. The alienation is compounded by the loss of civility in public discourse, and heightened by very shrill voices on social media. It seems that divisive walls are being erected everywhere.

Second, because of what is happening in our churches and Christian organisations. Division is one of Satan's strategies designed to hinder the advance of the gospel and the growth of the church. It's a deeply disturbing reality.

The widespread image of evangelicals, according to some writers, is one of people 'who cannot be expected to agree, either with each other or with the rest of the church on earth: people who are famous, indeed notorious, for eccentric individualism, for fighting and splitting, for dissenting and separating.'[3]

> Division is one of Satan's strategies designed to hinder the advance of the gospel and the growth of the church

Psalm 133 has the opening declaration, 'How good and how pleasant it is when God's people live together in unity!' In John Goldingay's commentary on this Psalm, he wrote, 'The most spectacularly unanswered prayer in world history is Jesus's prayer in John 17. Christian kinfolk live in breath-taking

2. Tim Marshall, *Divided: Why we're living in an age of walls* (London: Elliott and Thompson Ltd, 2018).
3. Quoted in J. I. Packer and Thomas C. Oden, *One Faith: The evangelical consensus* (Downers Grove, Ill.: InterVarsity Press, 2004), p. 14.

disharmony.'[4] We might not agree with the way Goldingay expresses this, but we all understand the sentiment he is expressing.

And third, there is the issue of our leadership response. Ephesians 4: 3 raises the question of whether we are making 'every effort to keep the unity of the Spirit'. There is an intensity and force about this exhortation as we'll see in a moment. It is a question posed by John Stott in his commentary that has been nagging many of us: 'Where, I ask myself, is this eagerness today? Is this an apostolic command we are guilty of largely ignoring?'[5]

So let's look at these verses, and consider them as they relate to four core issues: *calling, character, conviction, concern.*

> As a prisoner for the Lord, then, I urge you to live a life worthy of the calling you have received. Be completely humble and gentle; be patient, bearing with one another in love. Make every effort to keep the unity of the Spirit through the bond of peace. There is one body and one Spirit, just as you were called to one hope when you were called; one Lord, one faith, one baptism; one God and Father of all, who is over all and through all and in all. (Eph. 4: 1–6)

1. A calling to live by: *Ephesians 4: 1*

> As a prisoner of the Lord, then, I urge you to live a life worthy of the calling you have received.

Paul has provided three amazing chapters describing the foundations of God's saving work and his gracious calling of Jew and Gentile into the one new family of God. Now in chapter 4, he turns to practical exhortation. He is going to talk about how we live in the local church, how we behave in marriage, the family and the workplace, how we engage in everyday speech,

---

4. John Goldingay, *Psalms: Volume 3: Psalms 90–150*, Baker Commentary on the Old Testament Wisdom and Psalms (Ada, Mich.: Baker Academic, 2008), p. 569.
5. John Stott, *God's New Society: The Message of Ephesians* (Leicester: IVP, 1979), p. 154.

and how we confront spiritual warfare. So his appeal in the opening verse of chapter 4 introduces this practical teaching: live a life worthy of that calling.

What is the basis of our calling? We can select three verses from the earlier chapters of Ephesians which explain this.

First, **God's purpose**. Paul has already provided us with God's great mission statement at the beginning of his letter. The verses explain that God's purpose is: 'to bring unity to all things in heaven and on earth under Christ.' (1: 10) It is a remarkable verse which tells us where everything is heading: all things will be summed up to find their unity and completion in Jesus Christ. Paul uses a word from mathematics. When we add up, we place the total at the bottom, but the Greeks literally did 'add up', and they placed the total at the top. So Paul is underlining an amazing truth: God's purpose is that everything will be summed up to find its unity and completion in Christ. That is God's ultimate purpose.

Second, **God's people.** In the second chapter of Ephesians, Paul shows us that God has demonstrated that unity in the creation of a new family, or a new society: 'His purpose was to create in himself one new humanity . . .' (2: 15)

In context, the really big issue that Paul addresses is the division between Jew and Gentile. He declares that in Christ they are now members of the same family. We know that this was radical good news in Ephesus. The city was made up of people from many different backgrounds; it was a very plural culture. But now the church in Ephesus provided evidence of a unique reconciled community, crossing the boundaries of race, class and ethnicity.

Third, **God's pilot project.** In the light of Paul's teaching about God's purpose, he explains that the church is a model of the completed reconciliation of all things. I draw the language from a comment by Fred Bruce: 'The church appears to be God's pilot scheme for the reconciled universe of the future.'[6]

---

6. F. F. Bruce, quoted in Bruce Milne, *Dynamic Diversity* (Nottingham: IVP, 2006), pp. 24, 25. In his *The Epistle to the Ephesians* (Glasgow: Pickering & Inglis, 1961), pp, 16–18, Bruce

In fact, Paul explains that this is a powerful witness to God's purposes: 'so that through the church the manifold wisdom of God might now be made known to the rulers and authorities in the heavenly places.' (Eph. 3: 10 (ESV)) It might be hard to believe, but the local church—the redeemed and reconciled Christian community—testifies to everyone God's wisdom in the gospel and his purpose to restore all things in Christ. That must be the mission of our church.

Just as it was a radical statement in first century Ephesus, so it is in our world. As we have said, we live in a day of increasing tribalism and division. By contrast, one of the exciting features of Paul's teaching—also reflected in Luke's account in the book of Acts—is the way in which the gospel of Jesus Christ, preached in the power of the Spirit, dismantled the various alienations that were present in the first century. The Holy Spirit was breaking down barriers and creating a new society—a remarkable internationalism that didn't mean squashing the diversity, but that crossed the boundaries, removed the dividing walls, and created a new fellowship. In Christ the prejudices of culture, and gender, and ethnicity, and economic status were destroyed.

This is why, when we fail to live as we should, we give entirely the wrong message to the world outside. There is an obvious credibility gap when we affirm our unity and community, and yet fail to demonstrate that reality in our lives.

> In Christ the prejudices of culture, and gender, and ethnicity, and economic status were destroyed

amplified the point: 'In Ephesians the Church, the body of Christ, is a new community created by God to be the dwelling-place and vehicle of His Spirit, with a view to the consummation of His eternal purpose and the establishment of His dominion throughout all creation. . . . In this purpose of cosmic reconciliation the Church has an essential part to play, for the Church is herself God's masterpiece of reconciliation. . . . it is composed of men and women who have also been reconciled to one another through Christ. . . . In this reconciling work of His the Church has a service to perform, not only as God's masterpiece of reconciliation, but also as His instrument for bringing about the cosmic reconciliation which is His ultimate purpose.'

Some years ago, I paid my first visit to Bulgaria. I hadn't realised that this was the one European country that had reversed the usual cultural signals associated with 'yes' and 'no'. At that time, Bulgarians traditionally nodded for 'no', and shook their heads for 'yes'. I wish someone had told me this before I was due to preach. I struggled through my sermon with the congregation shaking their heads; the more passionately I preached, the more vigorously they shook their heads!

Of course, if we did this in our culture, we would be sending out two contradictory signals at the same time. And this is exactly the confusion generated when we Christians talk about unity. We are in danger of giving a mixed message—we declare that we are 'all one in Christ', but we say something different by our behaviour, by our failure to demonstrate that gospel reconciliation. This is why Paul begins with his appeal: '. . . I urge you to live a life worthy of the calling you have received.' (4: 1)

We come to Paul's next encouragement.

2. A character to display: *Ephesians 4: 2*

> Be completely humble and gentle; be patient, bearing with one another in love. (4: 2)

It is surely significant that the first implication of the universal gospel that Paul has described is a call for Christian character. God is saying: if you are part of this new humanity, this is how you should behave.

I read recently about a church meeting where two people disagreed strongly. In fact, one of them hit the other, leaving his fellow Christian unconscious on the floor. They had to call for an ambulance to take the man to hospital. The person writing about this event wondered what they would say in the minutes of the church meeting! He also wondered what the ambulance paramedics would say about it. It would be humorous were it not so tragic. It is too common in Christian community.

Have you ever noticed that, in Paul's list of the sins of the flesh in Galatians 5: 19–21, there is a strong emphasis on the divisive sins in the church—not just moral failure, but *relational failure*: 'hatred, discord, jealousy, fits of rage, selfish ambition, dissensions, factions and envy'.

Here in Ephesians 4 we notice two pairs: first, there are the two qualities which describe our attitude and behaviour towards others: 'humility and gentleness'. Humility was generally despised in Paul's day, but it is essential for how Christians should live together. The opposite of this attitude is pride, and this is always destructive in Christian fellowship. The early church father, Chrysostom, said that 'the greatest divider of the church is pride'.

Gentleness is not so common in our world either. Assertion, dominance, aggression, self-assurance, self-reliance—these are the words which have often been associated with secular leadership styles. The important issue here is that Christian character is modelled on Jesus Christ, not on the norms of our culture. Gentleness shows itself when we respond in Christlike ways in conflicts or disagreements in relationships. We should be slow to fight, and quick to make peace.

Then the second pair refer to the qualities which relate to how we respond to the behaviour of others towards us: 'patience and forbearance' (or bearing with one another in love). Again, this is just like Jesus. It's the opposite of fighting back. It means not getting irritated or angry. It is a deliberate choice to forgive someone.

The local church must model the gospel in the practical realm of attitudes and behaviour. This is a major issue in our churches, and once again it has implications for the credibility of our witness. I was struck by the strength of Bruce Milne's words when he commented on the well-known passage on unity in John 17:

> The biggest barriers to effective evangelism . . . are not so much outdated methods, or inadequate presentations of the

The local church must model the gospel in the practical realm of attitudes and behaviour

gospel, as realities like gossip, insensitivity, negative criticism, jealousy, backbiting, an unforgiving spirit, a 'root of bitterness', failure to appreciate others, self-preoccupation, greed, selfishness and every other form of lovelessness. These are the squalid enemies of effective evangelism which render the gospel fruitless and send countless thousands into eternity without a Saviour.[7]

Forbearance, or 'bearing with one another in love', is a fitting quality to sum up these essential relational qualities. Love binds everything and everyone together. I like Peter Lewis's suggestion that it is like the oil in the engine of your car. 'Love is the liquid engineering in your church. It prevents our personalities rubbing, our gifts grating, and our zeal overheating and bringing everything to a halt.'[8] These are Christlike qualities, since he was 'meek and lowly of heart'.

The letter of James speaks directly about the causes of fights and quarrels in the Christian community. He says that the reason for fracture in the church is because we demonstrate the opposite of the qualities we are looking at in Ephesians 4:2. 'For where you have envy and selfish ambition, there you find disorder and every evil practice.' (James 3: 16) He describes the chaos in relationships in the Christian community. By contrast, James says, '. . . the wisdom that comes from heaven is first of all pure; then peace-loving, considerate, submissive, full of mercy and good fruit, impartial and sincere.' (3: 17)

It is very similar to the qualities which Paul described when he wrote of the fruit of the Spirit in Galatians 5: 22, 23. People who express these qualities, through the Spirit's empowering presence, are slow to fight, they are submissive and open to reason, they are easily persuaded, and they defer to others rather than insist on their opinion or position. A church that has

---

7. Bruce Milne, *The Message of John*, The Bible Speaks Today (Leicester: IVP, 1993), pp. 250–251.
8. Peter Lewis, *Becoming Christlike* (Leicester: IVP, 2016), p. 81.

these qualities is a church marked by peace and co-operation, not strife and competition.

Breakdown and division are a very common cause of paralysis, but a harmonious, peaceful local church provides the atmosphere in which we can grow up as believers, becoming what God intended. This is a test of a healthy church—how we treat others, how we handle differences, how we respond to conflict and disagreement, how we care for awkward people. To grow a healthy church, we must ensure that the issue of character is prioritised within the teaching, training and modelling of every local church.

> Breakdown and division are a very common cause of paralysis, but a harmonious, peaceful local church provides the atmosphere in which we can grow up as believers

So first, Paul has described the foundations of our unity, and has urged us to live in line with that calling. Second, he has outlined the Christlike character that we must display if we are to grow in unity. He goes on to encourage commitment to unity, with a profound reminder of the God who creates true unity.

3. A conviction to believe: *Ephesians 4: 4–6*

> There is one body and one Spirit, just as you were called to one hope when you were called; one Lord, one faith, one baptism; one God and Father of all, who is over all and through all and in all. (4: 4–6)

It is important to see that Paul is not asking us to create unity, because that unity already exists. Rather, Paul is calling us to preserve a unity which arises from the nature of the God to whom we belong; it is built into the gospel which has saved us.

He refers to the oneness of God—Father, Son and Spirit—because God is three in one, and unity is the very essence of the Godhead. In these verses, there are seven unities: three unities within the Godhead, and then the four unities which they create.

There is **one Spirit** who produces the one body into which we are incorporated and the one hope to which we were called. As Paul says in 1 Corinthians 12: 13, the one indwelling Spirit means we are integrated into the one body.

Then there is **one Lord**, and so there is only one faith. We have come to believe in him and we are united in baptism. Our unity is a unity in the gospel of Jesus Christ and in our union with him.

And there is **one God and Father of all**. He creates the one family, and we belong to him. He is 'over all and through all and in all.' (4: 6)

The point is clear: everything about our faith is one. So how can we possibly live in division? Since you cannot divide or split the Godhead, you cannot divide the church. In fact, John Stott says in his commentary: 'The unity of the church is as indestructible as the unity of God himself. It is no more possible to split the church that it is to split the Godhead.'[9]

Well, I think I can now see a large question mark above your head! How is it that we display the opposite? How is it that we are so often divided?

We might have felt the same apparent ambiguity in the previous chapter when we looked at the challenge of holiness. In terms of status, the church is holy. Yet persistently in Scripture, we are called to grow in holiness. And Paul says the same with regard to unity. Because of the work of Father, Son and Spirit, the church is one. But here Paul is addressing the issue of practice as well as status—if *this* is true, then *here* is how should you behave.

Think of it like this. Margaret and I have three daughters. They are members of the Lamb family! They are fundamentally one. By God's grace, they get on very well together. But if they were in disagreement, or even alienated from each other in some way, they would need to remember their status: they are still members of the same family. They belong together, and they should demonstrate the Lamb family identity.

---

9. Stott, *God's New Society*, p. 151.

It's the same with the Christian family. One the one hand, there is an indestructible unity, formed by the Father, the Son and the Spirit. Jesus implied this in his prayer recorded in John 17, as he spoke about our shared life, our dwelling in him and in the Father. We are united to him and in him. Yet on the other hand, there is a unity which has to be maintained, a unity which has to be expressed. It is a unity that needs to grow, and a unity which must be demonstrated to the world. This is just as Jesus prayed: '. . . so that they may be brought to complete unity.' (John 17: 23)

Paul's Trinitarian statement is the fundamental conviction which underlies this unity. It is the *foundation* for our hope that Jesus' prayer will be answered, but it is also our *motivation* for change.

We come to our final verse.

4. A concern to strive for: *Ephesians 4: 3*

'Make every effort to keep the unity of the Spirit through the bond of peace.' (4: 3)

It is essential to catch the sense of urgency in this verse. It's not an easy phrase to translate, but the word Paul uses encapsulates several ideas—there is a sense of haste, of passion, even a sense of crisis. 'Make every effort to keep the unity of the Spirit' (NIV); '. . . be eager to maintain the unity of the Spirit' (ESV). In fact, it was translated by Karl Barth like this: 'Yours is the initiative! Do it now!'

Having looked at Paul's teaching in Ephesians, we can understand why there is such urgency. *Look at God's calling*—to be part of that new humanity, the pilot project that points to the reconciliation of all things in this universe! And then *look at the character* he requires, the qualities of humility, meekness and love which the Lord Jesus displayed. And then *look at the unities* which God himself, Father, Son and Spirit, has created!

In fact, these urgent verbs are found throughout the New Testament:

> I *appeal* to you, brothers and sisters, in the name of our Lord Jesus
> Christ, that all of you *agree with one another* in what you say and that
> there will be *no divisions among you*, but that you be *perfectly united
> in mind and thought.* (1 Cor. 1: 10)

> I *urge* you, brothers and sisters, to *watch out for those who cause
> divisions . . .* (Rom. 16: 17)

> *Strive* for full restoration, *encourage* one another, *be of one mind,* live
> in peace. (2 Cor. 13: 11)

> *Make every effort to live in peace* with everyone and to be holy; . . .
> (Heb. 12: 14)

> Let us therefore *make every effort* to do what leads to peace and to
> mutual edification. (Rom. 14: 19)

It is surely significant that, as Paul begins with the practical exhortations
in Ephesians chapters 4 to 6, this is the number-one priority. This has first
place. Nothing is more important for a local church than growing in unity.

> Let us therefore make every effort to do what leads to peace and to mutual edification

Of course, this is why disunity is so serious. Do you remember Paul's passionate appeal to the Corinthians? 'Don't you know that you yourselves are God's temple and that God's Spirit lives among you?' (1 Cor. 3: 16). This is not just a description of the Spirit who indwells individual Christians, but it has a corporate focus: it is a description of the church. Hence the sober warning which follows: 'If anyone destroys God's temple, God will destroy that person; . . .' (1 Cor. 3: 17).

Some years ago, I had regular contact with believers caught up in the violence and genocide between Hutu and Tutsi tribes in Rwanda and Burundi. With my colleagues in International Fellowship of Evangelical Students, I was very moved to hear that Christian young people had refused to take sides in that devastating ethnic conflict, and at the request of the Government, a group of Hutu and Tutsi Christians travelled the country together as a model of reconciliation. There was a cost, of course. In Rwanda, most of the staff and student leaders were killed during the genocide. But they knew that their primary identity was in Christ, and that they were therefore part of that one new humanity, the one family. Dividing along ethnic grounds was ruled out by that primary calling—to make every effort to keep the unity of the Spirit in the bond of peace.

The call to grow in unity leads to a mature and fruitful congregation. Paul goes on to explain this later in the chapter:

> . . . until we all reach unity in the faith and in the knowledge of the Son of God and become mature, attaining to the whole measure of the fullness of Christ. (Eph. 4: 13)

And how does this happen? Paul provides the answer: '. . . as each part does its work.' (4: 16) A healthy church, displaying unity, growth and maturity is the result of the proper functioning of every part of the body.

We look forward to the day when God will bring unity to all things, just as Ephesians 1 declares. But as God's pilot project, we must live out that vision in a fractured world. Let us encourage our churches to embrace these four themes: *a calling to live by, a character to display, a conviction to believe, and a concern to strive for.*

> 'Make every effort to keep the unity of the Spirit through the bond of peace.'

DISCUSSION AND APPLICATION

1. *Think of a situation of division or disagreement that you have experienced.*

    •   How might it have been different if the people involved had displayed the qualities mentioned in this passage—humility, gentleness, patience and forbearance?

2. *It is important to define the parameters of unity.*

    •   How do we determine what is necessary to affirm and what we can allow as legitimate difference?

    Take a look at Acts 15, and the story of the Council of Jerusalem. They determined what was primary (essential to the truth of the gospel) and what was secondary (important, but not something over which Christians should divide).

    •   How can you hold firmly to a matter of principle which might be secondary in terms of the gospel, while still enjoying warm fellowship with someone who sees things differently?

3. *Paul encourages congregations to be likeminded.*

    •   In what practical ways do you think a local church can cultivate among its members the common mind to which Paul refers in these two passages?

    Therefore if you have any encouragement from being united with Christ, if any comfort from his love, if any common sharing in the Spirit, if any tenderness and compassion, then make my joy complete by being like-minded, having the same love, being one in spirit and of one mind. (Phil. 2: 1, 2)

    May the God who gives endurance and encouragement give you the same attitude of mind toward each other that Christ Jesus had, so that with one mind and one voice you may glorify the God and Father of our Lord Jesus Christ' (Rom. 15: 5, 6).

4.   *Let's remember the radical manifesto of Galatians 3: 28:*

> 'There is neither Jew nor Gentile, neither slave nor free, nor is there male and female, for you are all one in Christ Jesus.'

- How do we dismantle tribalism?
- Is there something we can do to build bridges of fellowship in our church—crossing the barriers of class, race, gender and age?

5.   *We see in scripture that it is possible to disagree agreeably.*

- What qualities are needed for this to happen?

6.   *An important aspect of unity is strengthening partnerships.*

- On what foundation and in what ways can we express solidarity with other churches?
- What types of cooperation are possible?
- What partnerships can we build to express unity with believers in a different context from our own, whether in our city, our country, or around the world?

7.   *Spend a moment praying that the dynamic words we have looked at—'make every effort', 'be eager', 'strive', 'work hard'—will shape the commitment of your church to demonstrate the unity that God has achieved.*

CHAPTER 4

Growth through God's word[1]

Base passage: Nehemiah 8: 1–12

Some years ago the English clergyman, J. B. Phillips, was working on a paraphrase of the New Testament and explained that the experience was similar to working on the mains electricity of a house, but doing so with the electricity still switched on. It was a dynamic, electric experience! The book was 'live'; it was powerful and energizing. As Luther put it, 'The Bible is alive—it has hands and grabs hold of me, it has feet and runs after me.'

The Bible itself is full of dynamic descriptions of the word. Jeremiah said that God's word was like fire in his bones, or like a hammer that breaks a rock in pieces. Paul described it as the sword of the Spirit. The idea is repeated in Hebrews: 'living and active, sharper than any two-edged sword' (Heb. 4: 12). Jesus said that the word was the seed which produced a wonderful harvest.

And there is the intriguing story in Luke 24, when two disciples were walking home to Emmaus after the dramatic events of Jesus' crucifixion in Jerusalem. They didn't recognise Jesus, but he deliberately chose not to reveal himself, other than through the Bible: 'And beginning with Moses

---

1. This chapter arises from a workshop at the Brethren Training Network Consultation in 2018 at Dubuque, Iowa, USA, on the theme of strengthening Bible teaching in our churches. Its focus is therefore on the task of Bible exposition, but the principles drawn out from the account in Nehemiah 8 apply more widely, and will, I hope, help every reader in how to understand the Bible and explain it to others.

A more extensive treatment of these themes, based on the Nehemiah account, is to be found in my book, *Preaching Matters: Encountering the Living God* (Nottingham: IVP, 2014).

and all the prophets, he explained to them what was said in all the Scriptures concerning himself.' (Luke 24: 27)

In other words, it was through Scripture that they encountered the living Christ. The reason why our churches should be committed to listen to, understand and explain God's word is because we believe it has the same dynamic impact today. It transforms understandings and attitudes; it changes lives; it draws us into a living relationship with God.

> The reason why our churches should be committed to listen to, understand and explain God's word is because we believe it has the same dynamic impact today

There is a great example of this dynamic word in action in the account in Nehemiah 8. Our purpose in this chapter is especially to highlight the importance of Bible exposition for the health of our churches, but the themes we will draw out from this remarkable story are applicable to the many different settings where the Bible is read and explained—whether in youth groups, or home groups, or in personal reading. As we saw in chapter 1, growth in understanding God's word is critical to the wellbeing of every believer, and so we focus particularly on the task of preaching as we explore Nehemiah 8.

As we read the passage (Nehemiah 8: 1–12), it is good to ask, what are the elements in this account which demonstrate what is happening when the Bible is opened as it should be?

> . . . all the people came together as one in the square before the Water Gate. They told Ezra the teacher of the Law to bring out the Book of the Law of Moses, which the LORD had commanded for Israel.
>
> So on the first day of the seventh month Ezra the priest brought the Law before the assembly, which was made up of men and women and all who were able to understand. He read it aloud from daybreak till noon as he faced the square before the Water Gate in the presence

of the men, women and others who could understand. And all the people listened attentively to the Book of the Law.

Ezra the teacher of the Law stood on a high wooden platform built for the occasion. Beside him on his right stood Mattithiah, Shema, Anaiah, Uriah, Hilkiah and Maaseiah; and on his left were Pedaiah, Mishael, Malkijah, Hashum, Hashbaddanah, Zechariah and Meshullam.

Ezra opened the book. All the people could see him because he was standing above them; and as he opened it, the people all stood up. Ezra praised the LORD, the great God; and all the people lifted their hands and responded, 'Amen! Amen!' Then they bowed down and worshipped the LORD with their faces to the ground.

The Levites—Jeshua, Bani, Sherebiah, Jamin, Akkub, Shabbethai, Hodiah, Maaseiah, Kelita, Azariah, Jozabad, Hanan and Pelaiah—instructed the people in the Law while the people were standing there. They read from the Book of the Law of God, making it clear and giving the meaning so that the people understood what was being read.

Then Nehemiah the governor, Ezra the priest and teacher of the Law, and the Levites who were instructing the people said to them all, 'This day is holy to the LORD your God. Do not mourn or weep.' For all the people had been weeping as they listened to the words of the Law.

Nehemiah said, 'Go and enjoy choice food and sweet drinks, and send some to those who have nothing prepared. This day is holy to our Lord. Do not grieve, for the joy of the LORD is your strength.'

The Levites calmed all the people, saying, 'Be still, for this is a holy day. Do not grieve.'

Then all the people went away to eat and drink, to send portions of food and to celebrate with great joy, because they now understood the words that had been made known to them.

There are three key themes to look at as we consider the core elements of preaching the Bible. Under each of these three themes we will

- highlight key features of the Nehemiah account
- draw three implications for preachers
- suggest some contemporary challenges to which we must respond.

1. The word of God and the heart of preaching

The opening verse introduces us to a new section of the book, all to do with the spiritual restoration of God's people. The building of the walls is now over, but the true foundation for the restored community will be God's word. There are two features of the text which demonstrate that Ezra and Nehemiah saw the word as the foundation for all that was to follow.

Its centrality: the seventh month for God's people was a month of great religious festivity, and their first act was to call for the book. Verse 1 describes the grassroots' desire that the law should be read:

> All the people assembled before the Water Gate. They told Ezra the scribe to bring out the Book of the Law of Moses, which the Lord had commanded for Israel.

And the law commanded the attention of everyone—'all the people listened attentively' (v. 3). It retained its central place, day after day, right through to the end of the month. The word of God represented the foundation articles, the new constitution of the people of God. For a nation seeking its identity and shaping its programme of restoration, the word of God mattered. It was central. There is even something symbolic in the fact that it was not read in the Temple but, according to verse 3, 'He read it aloud from daybreak till noon as he faced the square before the Water Gate . . .'

Its authority: here it is simply to note the emphasis of verse 1:

> They told Ezra the scribe to bring out the Book of the Law of Moses, which the Lord had commanded for Israel.

Its human authorship is acknowledged on several occasions—the reading was from the books of Moses. But its divine authority is emphasised—the law of God, the revelation given by him. The law was 'teaching' or instruction from God himself. Without this sense of divine authority, it would simply be the veneration of a book. And that is the vital perspective for our own understanding of Scripture too. There is a wonderful explanation of this in 1 Thessalonians, where Paul describes the way in which the believers received the gospel:

> We thank God continually because, when you received the word of God, which you heard from us, you accepted it not as the word of men, but as it actually is, the word of God which is at work in you who believe. (1 Thess. 2: 13)

There are two significant themes here.

First, *its authority*: it is 'the word of God'. This is very emphatic in the way in which Paul wrote it. The message of the apostles is authoritative because it originates with God himself.

Second, *its power*: 'which is at work in you who believe'. It is powerful precisely because it is God's word. We shouldn't drive a wedge between the written word and the living God who speaks that word. By God's Spirit, it is powerful, life-giving, life-transforming. It 'goes on working'. It is not simply propositions, distant and cold, but a dynamic word that by the power of the Spirit turns us round to serve God, and shapes the way in which we are to live. That is the foundation for our authority, conviction and passion as those called to preach.

> It is not simply propositions, distant and cold, but a dynamic word that by the power of the Spirit turns us round to serve God, and shapes the way in which we are to live

Some implications:

1. Bible exposition must be centred on God's word

I spoke some while ago with a pastor in one of the Central Asian Republics. He said, 'I write my sermon and then look for a Bible passage to support it'. It is a surprisingly common strategy. But this is to use the Bible as a peg on which to hang our own thoughts. If we do this, we are not allowing the Bible to speak. But as we have seen from Nehemiah, the word must be centre stage. So we must 'preach on the passage, the whole passage, and nothing but the passage', as David Day has expressed it.[2] There are two important reasons why this should be so.

First, *the Bible passage establishes our authority*. Preaching is not authoritative because of our personality, our academic study, or our communication skills, but because of the authority of the God who speaks that word.

Second, *the Bible passage defines and limits the message*. It gives us the subject and shapes all we have to say. It is the architect's plan.

> Preaching is not authoritative because of our personality, our academic study, or our communication skills, but because of the authority of the God who speaks that word

2. Bible exposition must be immersed in God's word

If preaching is to have this biblical dynamic, then those of us who preach need to be wholeheartedly committed to immersing ourselves in Scripture. There are no short cuts. There are many other things that will crowd in to exclude the study, prayer and meditation which good preaching requires.

I have no doubt at all that it is a constant challenge. The apostles in the New Testament soon discovered that many things distracted them from the priority of the word and prayer, as we shall see in our next chapter, and that they needed to take action to ensure that first things were first (Acts 6: 1–7).

---

2. David Day, *A Preaching Workbook* (London: SPCK, 1998), p. 21.

The same commitment is underlined in Paul's encouragements in the Pastoral Epistles: 'Until I come, devote yourself to the public reading of Scripture, to preaching and to teaching . . . Be diligent in these matters; give yourself wholly to them, so that everyone may see your progress. Watch your life and doctrine closely.' (1 Tim. 4: 13, 15, 16).

3. Bible exposition must open up God's word

When we look at the New Testament words for preaching, it is clear that they point towards one fundamental matter: preaching is not announcing our own words in our authority, but proclaiming God's word with his authority. There are four word-groups which help us understand the nature of preaching. The most common word-group means to *declare as a herald*. Preaching is to proclaim the message which is given with the authority of the God who sends us. The message is not generated by the messenger, but it is given by God himself.

The second is related to *announcing the good news*. It is not used exclusively of the task of evangelism, though it includes that. Again, it is God's good news, not ours. The third group of words relates to the task of *witnessing or testifying to the facts*. And the fourth word, which is often translated *'teaching'*, is to lay out the facts as God has revealed them.

Notice that the emphasis is on the 'given-ness' of the message. We are to proclaim the *word of the Lord*.

Further, if we look at Paul's instructions to Timothy, we see how insistent he was that pastoral ministry involves faithful, urgent, proclamation of that word. So Paul presses home the point—our task is to proclaim the Bible. Nothing else will do, for nothing else reveals God's purposes, nothing else has such transforming power.

Good biblical preaching arises from an attitude of mind, a submissive approach to the Scriptures and to the God who has spoken that

> Good biblical preaching arises from an attitude of mind, a submissive approach to the Scriptures and to the God who has spoken that word

word. The style in which this is done or the structure which is used will vary greatly according to our culture, our tradition and our personality. But the core commitment is universal.

Some challenges:

Addressing Biblical illiteracy and the loss of confidence in the Bible

Some years ago the British church survey, 'Taking the Pulse', by the Bible Society and the Evangelical Alliance, revealed a loss of confidence in the Bible, and therefore loss of its centrality in the churches. One of the questions was: 'Do secularists like Richard Dawkins affect our confidence in the Bible?', and a quarter of church leaders admitted that the attack of militant atheism affected their confidence. Further, 40% of churchgoers felt their confidence in the Bible was undermined by this trend. There are other troubling statistics: 70% of churchgoers indicated that they didn't read the Bible outside of church events or on a regular basis.

We know that, in many countries, this generation has limited biblical understanding. In the USA, according to the Institute for Bible Reading, 87% of churchgoers say 'what they need most from their church is help in understanding the Bible in depth'. This is cited by Kevin Vanhoozer in his significant book entitled, *Hearers and Doers*[3], which helps churches truly to understand and live the truth of the Bible. In chapter 1, we also mentioned the book, *Grounded in the Gospel*,[4] with its encouragement to develop accessible teaching that introduces the key biblical themes every believer must come to understand.

Restoring the centrality of the Bible in church life

The marginalisation of preaching is just one aspect of the marginalisation of the Bible. So we need to work hard to restore its central place—in our homes, our church life, our small groups, and in our preaching.

---

3. Kevin Vanhoozer, *Hearers and Doers: A Pastor's Guide to Making Disciples Through Scripture and Doctrine*, (London: Lexham Press, 2019).
4. See chapter 1, footnote 5, p. 16.

Deuteronomy 6 reminds us that our love for God will be expressed by our determination to bring his word into the centre of our life, our families and our Christian communities:

These commandments that I give you today are to be upon your hearts. Impress them on your children. Talk about them when you sit at home and when you walk along the road, when you lie down and when you get up. Tie them as symbols on your hands and bind them on your foreheads. Write them on the doorframes of your homes and on your gates. (Dt. 6: 6–9)

> Our love for God will be expressed by our determination to bring his word into the centre of our life, our families and our Christian communities

2. The teacher and the work of preaching

Next, we turn to Ezra and his team of helpers. There are several significant features of their service that day in Jerusalem.

Making it accessible: the text is extremely clear at this point. If God's word was to be the foundation for their families, their day-to-day living, and their society, then it had to be clear, it had to be accessible to everyone. 'All the people assembled as one man . . .' (Neh. 8: 1). Ezra read before the assembly 'which was made up of men and women and all who were able to understand.' (v. 2, repeated in v. 3); then 'all the people could see him . . .' (v. 5) Every attempt was made to ensure that everyone had access to God's word.

Making it clear: the account shows us the stress placed on understanding, not only the texts we've mentioned ('all who were able to understand', which must have meant men, women and children), but the emphasis on making the content of the law clear. So verse 8 tells us: 'giving the meaning so that the people could understand what was being read.'

The reason for the people's response is recorded in verse 12: '. . . because they now *understood* the words that had been made known to them.'

The fact that the reading of the law was not just for priests or Levites, and that Ezra chose the city centre rather than the temple, strengthens the sense that the law needed to be heard and understood by everyone. It was—and is—God's word for all.

Working together: Nehemiah 8: 4 demonstrates that Ezra chose a group of others to help him with the reading, and verses 7 and 8 show that teams helped with the interpretation and explanation.

In some cultures, the preacher or the pastor can sometimes come across as the professional, the expert. But the important task with which we are charged is not only to teach, but through our handling of the Bible also to help others to understand how to enjoy Scripture. In that sense, we are not just providing a good meal; we are aiming to help others know how to prepare a meal for themselves. We need to find ways to engage others in this task. Many churches around the world now have small preachers' groups which meet regularly to work together in preparing their messages and in planning the teaching diet for the church.

> We are not just providing a good meal; we are aiming to help others know how to prepare a meal for themselves

Implications for preachers:

4. Bible exposition must be focussed
As we have seen, Ezra and Nehemiah were concerned that everyone should understand. Biblical preaching must focus on this urgent priority too. It begins, of course, with the preacher working hard on the Bible passage. I like the way Eugene Peterson expresses it: 'Exegesis is loving God enough to stop and listen carefully to what he says.'

But more than this. For preaching to be effective, there is also one important aspect to understanding the passage: to understand its *primary message*. What is the big idea of this passage, as we often say? What is its melodic line? What is the *heartbeat*—the key idea which is pumping the blood round, the life-giving force of this passage of Scripture?

In order to understand the passage and to communicate its meaning to our congregation, it is essential to have discovered this big idea, the main theme which will dominate our message.

For me, this is the most important part of my preparation. Unless I am clear about this, I will not be able to preach with conviction and with passion. It is this which is central to Bible exposition. It is exposing the fundamental meaning of this passage, opening up its force and power, showing people how it applies to them and urging them to accept it and respond to it. That is preaching with focus.

> It is exposing the fundamental meaning of this passage, opening up its force and power

5. Bible exposition must be clear

Ezra and his team worked hard at the task of making the reading of the Scriptures clear. We have seen the different ways in which they did this, doubtless involving translation, interpretation, discussion and explanation. The biblical preacher must do the same. Sadly, we know this is not always the case. Sometimes, there is a fair amount of fog in the pulpit. Some preachers leave people less clear after the sermon than they were before it!

Related to this: we will help our listeners to understand better what we are saying if we are clear in the way in which we present our message. Some form of structure is nearly always helpful. A clear structure helps the preacher to organize his thoughts and present them in persuasive and memorable ways. And a good clear structure helps the listener to concentrate and to focus on the Bible passage, and hopefully to remember the key points later.

The goal is exactly the same as it was for Ezra's team of helpers who 'helped the people to understand . . . They gave the sense, so that the people understood the reading.' (Neh. 8: 7–8 (ESV)) That is what clear preaching does.

6. Bible exposition must be relevant
As well as making the text of the Bible accessible and clear, we must engage not only with Scripture, but with our listeners. So we work hard to present the material, not only in a way that can be grasped, but also in ways that resonate with their situation. As we prepare to preach, we must spend time not only thinking about *what we are preaching about*, but also thinking about *who we are preaching to.*

If we are going to communicate the dynamic force of any Bible passage, then our application of it must connect with the needs that we perceive in our congregation, or the challenges of our culture, or the circumstances of our hearers. The great preachers of the Bible—the prophets, the apostles, and Jesus himself—were all concerned to contextualize the message in ways which directly addressed their hearers. But we should note that application *first of all* arises from the questions and the challenges and the encouragements of the Bible passage itself.

Some challenges:

Restoring confidence in preaching
It is true that preaching these days doesn't get a good press. Pulpits can be seen as platforms for self-appointed bullies. Some dictionary definitions don't help: 'to preach' is 'to discourse on moral or religious topics, especially in a tiresome manner'. But it seems that there is also a hunger, and in some countries it is specially among the young. A recent survey about church life made reference to a 15-year-old who was asked, 'what would your church lose if it lost the sermon?' and he replied, 'The congregation'. He was right. The survey indicated that young people are definitely not anti-preaching, but are keen to understand and to live the truth. There is a welcome seriousness in the rising generation, for which we must thank God and to which we must respond.

Strengthening training

It is happening, but much more needs to be done, specially through non-formal approaches. We often recommend the use of small preachers' groups—in the work of Langham Preaching, these are called preachers' clubs, and there are thousands of them around the world. This can be a group from different churches, or a group within one church. I know of preachers from a variety of evangelical churches in a Colombian city who meet together to prepare from the same passage, and then preach that same passage in their different churches on Sunday.

Many of us have been members of a preachers' club in our own church—with the regular preachers and the youth workers and some home group leaders, perhaps meeting over breakfast on Saturday, working together to understand and apply the passage. Often, preachers are lonely, and we need to work together, just as they did in Nehemiah's day.

Finally, we come to the third main element of the story in Nehemiah 8. The word was being read and also carefully explained. But as we have said, the word of God is dynamic—it has an effect. Something was happening to the hearers.

3. The congregation and the purpose of preaching

We read not only about the role of the teachers, but also the active participation of the congregation.

First, they were expectant

They were eager to hear the word. To begin with, we see in Nehemiah 8: 1 that the initiative was with the people who called on Ezra to bring out the book. Jim Packer makes the surprising suggestion that it must have been like the crowd at a rock concert: 'Imagine an impatient audience as a rock concert picking up the chant, "We want Ezra, we want Ezra", saying it over and over, louder and louder, and you get some idea of the feelings being expressed.'[5]

That same sense of eagerness and expectancy is expressed in verse 3: 'all the people listened attentively'; and verse 5, as the people stood up when the book was opened, and verse 13: everyone gathered 'to give attention to the words of the Law.' And it reminds us too that there is little to be gained from reading the Bible without such expectancy. Jesus' own ministry was frustrated when there was no expectancy on the part of his hearers. He began to teach in the synagogue and he was met with cynicism and incredulity. Expectant faith is the soil in which God's word will bear fruit, and that is a lesson throughout our Christian life.

> Expectant faith is the soil in which God's word will bear fruit

Second, they were serious

Here is a further sign of their spiritual hunger. They were ready to cope with all kinds of inconvenience in order to hear this word. Here the Water Gate congregation stood from daybreak to noon (v. 3)—for at least 5 hours, without a coffee-break in sight—because they longed to hear and understand what God had to say to them.

Then we read in verse 6: 'Ezra praised the Lord, the great God; and all the people lifted their hands and responded, Amen! Amen! Then they bowed down and worshipped the Lord with their faces to the ground.'

Maybe there is something to learn from the attitude of the people in Jerusalem that day: a longing for God to speak as they lifted up their hands; an attitude of reverence and respect as they bowed with their faces to the ground. Perhaps these attitudes are pre-requisites to understanding God's word and coming into his presence. Indeed, the verse is important

---

5. J. I. Packer, *A Passion for Faithfulness* (London: Hodder & Stoughton, 1995), p. 150.

in reminding us that we don't venerate the book as such: its purpose is to bring us into the presence of its author, the Lord, the great God.

So Nehemiah 8 demonstrates one important element of true teaching—it should bring us into God's presence. It mediates an encounter not merely with truth, but with God himself.

Third, they were obedient

Finally, we notice the result. The people experienced God's word in such a way that it called for a response at a variety of levels. Verse 9 shows the initial response: 'For all the people had been weeping as they listened to the words of the Law.' Their first hearing of the law provoked within the people a sense of contrition as they realised that their lives had failed to match up to the standards which God had set. But intriguingly, Ezra and Nehemiah move quickly to set that failure within the wider context of God's purposes for his people. And with the encouragement of the leaders, the people went to celebrate, to eat and drink 'with great joy' (v. 12). They had come to realise that it was God's desire to bless them, having seen this from all that had been read—'they now understood the words that had been made known to them.' (v. 12)

So the rest of chapters 8 and 9 demonstrate the impact of the word on the people. The prayer moves towards an expression of covenant renewal. They were ready for action. They wanted to live their lives in conformity with God's word, to demonstrate in their community that they belonged to him.

That's the significance of the sequence of these chapters. It is hearing God's word, celebrating God's goodness, knowing God's grace, and then obeying God's laws. It is truth in action. As we have already seen, truth is dynamic and life changing. We are called to *do the truth*, not simply to believe it.

Implications for preachers:

7. Bible exposition must call for change

Effective preaching calls for a response. All preaching must be transformational preaching. We know that Jesus left no room for neutrality or boredom when he preached. And in his record of various sermons preached in the book of Acts, Luke often describes how the people reacted, not with passivity, but with joyful acceptance, or alarm, or amazement, or even antagonism.

> **All preaching must be transformational preaching**

Preaching is not just to inform or instruct. It seeks to produce transformation of life. As Paul said to the Roman hearers,

> But thanks be to God that . . . you have come to obey from your
> heart the pattern of teaching that has now claimed your allegiance.
> (Rom. 6: 17)

The aim is to make God's word clear so that, by the Holy Spirit, people understand it in their own situation and then obey it. Preaching has the purpose of transformation.

8. Bible exposition must engage the listener

Jesus was particularly insistent that his audience truly heard what he was saying: 'Let anyone with ears to hear listen!' That seems to have been one of his characteristic sayings (Mark 4: 9, 23; Luke 8: 8).

Hearers need help in listening, and we should learn from the response of God's people throughout Scripture—expecting an encounter with God, ready to respond to his word and open to be changed by its power. Preaching should be a dynamic and a divine event.

> **Preaching is not just to inform or instruct. It seeks to produce transformation of life**

As Luther said: 'I just threw the Bible into the congregation and the word did the work.'

9. Bible exposition must proclaim God's grace in Christ
Nehemiah 8 demonstrates how the reading of the book of the law exposed the sin of the people (so they wept), but pointed them to the mercy of God (so they rejoiced). Then, in Nehemiah 9, the people confessed their sin, enjoyed God's grace, and renewed their commitment to him. Biblical preaching must always do the same. It must be grace-filled. And for us, standing now in the light of the New Testament, to preach grace, we must preach Christ.

Luther used to describe Scripture as the cradle in which we will find the baby. Its purpose is not to draw attention to itself, but to the person of Jesus. For the Scriptures, both Old and New Testaments, point to Jesus Christ. We must remember the twin priorities of explaining the word clearly and presenting Christ faithfully.

All preaching must be biblical preaching. And biblical preaching will be gospel-centred, empowered by the Spirit's energies, and will call for radical change.

Some challenges:

The need for double listening
There is an urgent need for application. This means listening to Scripture and also listening to the challenges in our world. We need to understand both the pastoral needs within our congregation, and also the uncertainties and confusion of our culture. We are then able to build the bridge from the Bible passage to the world of our day.

The need for integrity
Ezra has been central in the Nehemiah story. What made him such a remarkable figure? It is summed up in a pithy expression found in Ezra 7: 10.

> For Ezra had devoted himself to the study and observance of the Law
> of the LORD, and to teaching its decrees and laws in Israel.

The one dominant verb—'devoted'—describes his commitment to three things, described by the verbs: 'study, observe, teach'. He had set his heart and mind fully on that essential sequence—his own *study* of the truth led to his *doing* the truth, which only then led to his *teaching* the truth.

And here we come to a fundamental element in the dynamics of Bible exposition: *the word must be embodied* in the life of the preacher.

We have tackled this already in chapter 2, and so we will not elaborate. But we know there is sometimes a loss of credibility in preaching because of the way in which we fail to live the life. Preachers not only need to heed the usual advice of practising what we preach: perhaps we should only 'preach what we practise'! I realize that to do so will drastically reduce the length and variety of my sermons, but it is at the heart of integrity, and essential for the authentic preaching of God's word.

> Perhaps we should only 'preach what we practise'

These then are the dynamics of God's word at work. They demonstrate why Bible exposition is used by God's Spirit the world over, whatever the culture and whatever the personality of the preacher. True biblical preaching is a divine and therefore a dynamic event, as the Scriptures are opened and lives are transformed.

Few things are more important for growing healthy churches.

DISCUSSION AND APPLICATION

1.   *We have seen the importance of working together.*
   - In what ways can the preachers in your church encourage one another?

   - Have you considered a preachers' group which can meet regularly, working on Bible passages together, sharing ideas for application and illustration, planning a short preaching series together etc.?

2.   *We have seen the importance of expounding the Bible.*
   - In what ways can you encourage regular reading and study of Scripture within your preaching team?

   - Are there any reading schemes you could use, or any books or other resources you can share?

3.   *It is important to think about the teaching 'diet' in your church.*
   - Is there a good balance of Old and New Testament material?

   - As you reflect on the needs within the congregation or the challenges in your society, are there areas of teaching that would be important to consider?

4.   *Bible teaching opportunities in the church.*
   - In what ways can you encourage those who might not be teachers at main church gatherings, but who have to explain the Bible in youth programmes, children's work, women's meetings and similar programmes?

   - Are there ways in which they can be helped in their task of preparation, or given some training, or receive some feedback and encouragement?

5.   *Planning for the future.*
   - In what ways can you encourage the next generation of preachers in your church?

CHAPTER 5

Growth and change[1]

Base passage: Acts 6: 1–7

T he story of the Bible is a story of change. Whether it is the over-
arching narrative of creation, fall, redemption and new creation, or
the dynamic story of the planting and nurturing of churches in the book
of Acts, or the personal call for repentance and faithful obedience, positive
change is the necessary dynamic. The Christian life begins with a profound
change which we call 'conversion'. It is a radical change of allegiance which
is the start of a continuous process of change for the individual disciple and
for the Christian community.

All dimensions of growth in the local church inevitably involve change,
but whereas growth is usually welcomed, change is viewed with suspicion.
We often feel uneasy about change in the church, because it can so easily
become a major cause of division. A
small and apparently insignificant change
can provoke surprisingly fierce reactions.
Even when there is substantial agreement
regarding change, it inevitably introduces
some measure of stress and discomfort.

> Whereas growth is usually
> welcomed, change is
> viewed with suspicion

Some of us are so deeply affected
by change that it takes on crisis proportions. Reactions within a typical

---

1. Part of this chapter first appeared in *Essentially One: striving for the unity God loves*
(Nottingham: IVP, 2020), chapter 9, and Partnership expresses gratitude to the publisher
for permission to reproduce it in the present volume.

congregation will vary: psychologists use words like 'adaptation', 'mastery', 'coping' and 'defence' to describe our responses, and efforts to 'manage' change have produced a torrent of books and seminars. It seems none of us can escape it, and few of us welcome it.

Faithful and contemporary

The church is called to combine two qualities in her life and ministry which should never be divorced. First, the New Testament urges us to be *faithful* to the gospel. There is no need to renew or change the Good News with which we have been entrusted. Rather we are to demonstrate an unswerving commitment to the 'faith once for all revealed to the saints.' (Jude 1: 3) We are to defend it, preserve it, and to guard it. It is this commitment which makes us 'conservative evangelicals'. As we read Paul's letters, we see that there is no question about his faithfulness to the gospel. It is an absolute, a certainty—in his day and ours—even if the relativism of our culture rejects such a claim and appeals for a more 'tolerant' and flexible attitude.

Yet, at the same time, Christians are living in a society which is constantly changing. Our congregations are changing, whether in age profile, in pastoral needs, or in attitudes and values. The tastes of each generation are different from the previous one. 'Felt needs' change; the community where we live will change. In other words, the *context* for our proclamation of the unchanging gospel will change. Understanding that context is central to being effective within it.

So, while the gospel remains the same, and our commitment to it should hold steady, we shall need constant renewal of our methodology. This is not simply a matter of being contemporary in our evangelism. It is also true of our church structures and our approach to Christian ministry. Whether it is patterns of leadership, or worship, or issues of structure—home groups, care for children, ministry to women—Scripture allows considerable room for manoeuvre.

For example, the New Testament seems deliberately vague about the role of deacons. What do they do? We are not told. We are given a list of qualities, the qualifications to look for in someone who is to serve the church in this way; but it seems the Holy Spirit avoided recording details of a job description, so that we make the application according to each culture and generation. There is similar flexibility in New Testament ecclesiology with regard to many aspects of leadership, worship, evangelism, and church structure.

This enables each congregation, in whatever culture or age it is witnessing, to sustain its commitment to the unchanging primary truth of the gospel, while living out its calling as the body of Christ in a way which will be entirely appropriate for its cultural setting. We are to be *faithful* in our commitment to the unchanging God and his reliable word, and *contemporary* in our commitment to see that message transforming today's men and women.

Change and stability

In chapter 1, we looked at the dimensions of spiritual growth from Colossians 2. As we think about change, there is an interesting paradox in the verses we examined. In Colossians 2: 7, Paul indicates that we need to be *rooted* in Christ (and therefore stable) and also *built up* in him (and therefore changing). We can cope best with change in our lives when our identity is tied to Christ. If we have a stability that arises from a deep and secure relationship with him, we are then able to respond to change with steady faith and hope

> We can cope best with change in our lives when our identity is tied to Christ

rather than with fear. And this is the essence of mature Christian living: the word 'disciple' implies a willingness to learn, to change.

The church as the body of Christ must change. All of the analogies in Ephesians 4 and 1 Corinthians 12 point to the fact that the church is a living organism, and if the body is healthy, it will grow. Yet we have already acknowledged that change is greeted differently by different people, and it is important in our pastoral care of a congregation to recognise this. There are issues related to age, temperament and social background which can influence how change is handled in the church.

It is a mistake to imagine that older people always find change more difficult to cope with. It is frequently more to do with temperament and background. Nevertheless, it is the experience of many churches that change can become more demanding, more difficult to manage, as a congregation becomes older or more fixed in its membership. Too often, they feel alienated in the process of change, and we need to devote special care to those who could, with help, prayerfully support the growth and progress of the church.

Then we know that the local church, like every human organisation, is blessed by diverse personality types. While the diversity can be frustrating at times, generally it is part of what makes life both entertaining and en-riching. There are many ways in which this is seen. Some of us prefer to take our holidays in the same place year after year; others of us are bored if it's ever the same place twice. Or take the furniture in your front room—some people rearrange it every month, others wouldn't dream of disturbing a long-established domestic setting. Neither is right or wrong; we are just different. Similarly, if your job involves constant evaluation, the researching of new methods, and frequent adjustment to change, you are much more likely to think the same way in the church.

There is no doubt that a resistant stance to change can become a deep-set attitude. We frequently encounter confused commitments within congregations as well as among church leaders. In his best-selling biography *The Railway Man,* Eric Lomax recalls a visit to a Scottish church. 'The oldest members were immensely bitter and obsessed with status. If newcomers or visitors occupied a pew which an older member felt that he or she had a claim to, the interlopers were the object of furious resentment. These were petty divisions, petty angers, small minds'. I am glad that he added, 'For all that they made me feel welcome.'[2]

This kind of temperamental conservatism needs to be acknowledged and handled wisely. It should not be ignored or trampled over. Whether to do with age or temperament, it is a pastoral issue; and Christian leaders introducing change are not to be ruthless managers but empathetic pastors who understand the emotions felt by our fellow believers.

Lessons from a crisis

There is an additional factor that can impact how change is received, and that is to do with social or ethnic background. It was clearly a significant issue for the early Christian communities, and one example is the account in Acts 6 of the apostles' response to an urgent need in the community.

> In those days when the number of disciples was increasing, the Hellenistic Jews among them complained against the Hebraic Jews because their widows were being overlooked in the daily distribution of food. So the Twelve gathered all the disciples together and said, 'It would not be right for us to neglect the ministry of the word of God in order to wait on tables. Brothers and sisters, choose seven men from among you who are known to be full of the Spirit and wisdom. We will turn this responsibility over to them and will give our attention to prayer and the ministry of the word.' This proposal pleased the whole group. They chose Stephen, a man full of faith and of the Holy Spirit; also Philip, Procorus, Nicanor, Timon, Parmenas, and Nicolas from Antioch, a convert to Judaism. They presented these men to the apostles, who prayed and laid their hands on them. So the word of God spread. The number of disciples in Jerusalem increased rapidly, and a large number of priests became obedient to the faith. (Acts 6: 1–7)

---

2. Eric Lomax, *The Railway Man* (London: Vintage, 1996), p. 34.

It is strangely comforting to realise that the early Christians were human just like us—a row was brewing. A complaint arose against the apostles. Food was supposed to be shared among needy people, and the widows of the church were amongst the desperately poor. However, the newcomers to Jerusalem from a Greek and provincial background felt neglected, and tempers were running high. They saw this neglect as an expression of discrimination. The widows from the majority culture—the Hebraic Jews— were apparently being favoured over the minority group of Hellenistic Jews.

It was clearly a multi-layered problem: widows were feeling overlooked; the minority group to which they belonged thought that this neglect reflected favouritism towards the majority culture; and, to add a further layer of complexity, the apostles had a great deal on their plate, but insufficient resources to manage the situation. They clearly realized that the problems could easily lead to division within the community and that it was important to act if the situation were not to deteriorate still further.

How change was introduced

i) Identifying the issues

> So the Twelve gathered all the disciples together . . . (Acts 6: 2)

First, the leaders take a simple but significant action in bringing the believers together. They quickly understood the needs of the minority group and the urgency of addressing the situation, as well as the importance of sustaining prayer and the ministry of the word.

Most of our churches have majority and minority cultures. These cultures might sometimes be racial or ethnic, but they can also be of other kinds. Often, they are reflected in social class. In some countries, large city-centre churches are predominantly middle class, which means some people feel marginalized. Some city churches have a majority of single people in their congregation and these majority groups may also divide into other small groups, whether those from abroad, students, professionals, young people at school or unemployed people. But other churches have a majority of families, and the culture of the church is such that those who don't quite fit can easily feel excluded. Then churches often have generational differences, which can also represent majority and minority groups, sometimes in unhealthy ways.

The majority/minority issue can be a cause of apparent favouritism and complaint, as it was here in the early church. The foundations for preventing discrimination are expressed in James 2, and this applies to individuals or minorities in contexts of racial, social, class or language differences within our congregations. We need to do all we can to prevent any drift towards discrimination or favouritism. Similarly, the minority culture in the church needs to seek God's grace and patiently express those needs and objections to discrimination, avoiding the grumbling and the potential division that can follow.

> We need to do all we can to prevent any drift towards discrimination or favouritism

ii) Listening carefully

One of the questions raised for us by the passage is, who are we overlooking in our church? Are there marginalized groups being neglected? This is not always easy to detect because some of us are not so good at picking up the voices of the minority. Listening is a vital skill in pastoral leadership, especially when tackling disagreements. The account shows the wisdom of the apostles, who heard, understood, and then acted. There is no sign of a defensive response, but of an empathetic engagement with the issue. Listening is not always the first reaction of those who are the reformers, keen to press ahead with new initiatives, but sometimes insufficiently attuned to the cry of those on the periphery of the fellowship.

> Listening is a vital skill in pastoral leadership, especially when tackling disagreements

For good listening to happen, discussion is needed at all levels to enable members of the church family to express ideas, concerns and hopes. In my experience of change in a local context, we benefited greatly from wise leaders who sought to encourage careful listening at many levels—in personal conversations, in home groups, at church meetings, through literature and (very important) over meals. Meeting together in someone's home is a much more conducive environment for discussing differences than sitting in rows in a cold church building. At each stage, pastoral gentleness and sensitivity are needed as we listen and seek to understand.

Compassionate understanding is a vital part of identifying the issues behind disagreement. I recall an occasion in a church where I served when a member of the congregation reacted unexpectedly to a proposed reorganization of the chair layout. What appeared to us to be a harmless and simple adjustment led her to react with a surprising depth of feeling. I eventually discovered that she had always sat in the same place. Her customary seat had become associated with her late husband and other family members who had attended in the past. The emotional attachment meant a great deal to her, so hers was a reaction that had to be understood. For her, change meant disorientation; she was someone for whom we needed to care.

iii) Identifying priorities

> We . . . will give our attention to prayer and the ministry of the word. (6: 3, 4)

The apostles recognized the tension, both cultural and social, which needed to be resolved. They also recognized the danger that they could become preoccupied with the wrong ministry, so they clearly identified priorities. This is a vital principle for keeping a church on track: where do we want to get to? What are the main priorities which should shape the proposed change and the manner in which it should be introduced? How can leaders ensure they are not distracted from their primary tasks?

The apostles realised that prayer and the ministry of the word were the essential twin priorities of their ministry, and we know that these are vital for a healthy church. The important issue was not only that this was recognized, but also that the apostles saw the need for delegating tasks to ensure that their main priority was protected. Wise leaders identify priorities and deploy the good gifts of others to ensure that needs are addressed and growing work is well managed.

> **Wise leaders identify priorities and deploy the good gifts of others to ensure that needs are addressed and growing work is well managed**

iv) Creating ownership

> Brothers and sisters, choose seven men from among you who are known to be full of the Spirit and wisdom. We will turn this responsibility over to them . . . This proposal pleased the whole group. (6: 3, 5)

After assessing the needs, the apostles encouraged ownership of the problem. The believers themselves were called upon to exercise their wisdom in effecting the needed change. Everyone was involved in the process. They were to choose seven men full of the Spirit, doubtless including some who were members of the group against whom the majority were apparently discriminating.

Again, this is instructive. A healthy and unified church is one in which there is a sense of ownership. The believers were taken seriously. Involving them would have limited the sense of alienation and defused the atmosphere of conflict. It is true of most organizations, the church included, that if people have a limited role in the decision-making, then collectively

> **A healthy and unified church is one in which there is a sense of ownership**

they have great power to subvert or ignore changes that they don't wish to accept.

Nick Mercer once provided a useful illustration, when he suggested that sudden change is a bit like having a baby without being pregnant for nine months. The leaders have spent many hours and days in discussion, in the gestation of an idea. Then the 'baby' is suddenly presented at a church meeting which has forty-five minutes to make up its mind. No wonder there are so many unhappy births. The congregation must share in the pregnancy if it is to be a healthy baby.

Inclusion is essential for managing change and building unity. In a context of division, Paul encouraged the Philippians to be 'like-minded' (Phil. 2: 2). Although this idea is associated with unanimity in the gospel, it is also vital to the harmony of relationships. Encouraging involvement in as many ways as possible will help people to come to a common mind concerning what the church is seeking to achieve. True fellowship can be maintained by helping everyone to feel involved, as well as by the spirit in which any differences of opinion are discussed. This has been summed up by the phrase 'Nothing about us without us', which expresses the desire for ownership and involvement.

One of the most common signals of problems ahead can be heard over coffee or in home groups: 'Look at what *they're* trying to do now!' The polarized 'them/us' language demonstrates that there is little sense of ownership or mutuality. By contrast, the account in Acts 6 demonstrates a healthy commitment to delegation and ownership.

In this context, it is worth thinking about transparency. Articulating the concerns and acknowledging the problems are basic to preventing divisive positioning, and so it is important for difficulties to be brought out into the open. Almost everyone is affected by some of the changes that might be introduced, and they have to be able to express their fears, their possible opposition, their uncertainties or even their resentment. It takes time and patience, but it is healthy to encourage such openness. Too often, we think that differences of opinion can't be constructive, but understanding these responses also gives us the opportunity to modify plans or compromise on when and how they are implemented.

It is also helpful to explore the reasons for any resistance. People need to be helped to express their concern, perhaps their sense of loss, even their shock, fear or anger. We should try to prevent the development of quiet pockets of resistance which work undercover and which create a sense of fracture in the Christian community. It is far healthier to encourage everyone to express their views and feelings. Unfounded rumours are unhelpful distractions which gain currency rapidly. So the time-consuming effort of sharing our concerns widely with the whole church, communicating the *why* as clearly as possible, is essential—both to respect the congregation as God's family and to gain wider wisdom and prayerful solidarity.

Some churches have worked hard to strengthen ownership and transparency. While recognizing the necessity of discussing pastoral matters in confidence, some churches invite various members of the congregation to join some leadership discussions. Sometimes churches publish edited minutes of leaders' meetings as a way of helping the church family to pray regularly for leaders, to welcome comments and to demonstrate that there are no secrets. When a particular change is being considered, it is sensible to draw together interested groups early on in the process, which is all part of building trust and respecting fellow brothers and sisters.

v) Confirming change

> They presented these men to the apostles, who prayed and laid hands on them. (6: 6)

Spiritual leadership is vital for healthy church growth, as well as for maintaining the unity of the Spirit in the bond of peace. We often note that the seven who were called upon to help with the administrative duties of caring for the widows, across all groups, were 'full of the Spirit and wisdom' (6: 3). Stephen was 'full of faith and of the Holy Spirit' (6: 5).

Here, it is important to remember the New Testament teaching about the interdependence of the body. In whichever capacity we serve the Lord and his church, whether in the ministry of the word or waiting on tables, we need the enabling of God's Spirit. Of course, different levels of spiritual maturity and experience will be needed for certain tasks. But one of the reasons for so much conflict in our churches relates to the failure to ensure that all those carrying responsibility are spiritually qualified and are expressing the wisdom and commitment that is needed.

The apostles publicly dedicated these fellow workers to the task, praying and laying hands on them. This not only confirmed the choice of individuals, but was also a declaration of mutual accountability. In God's presence, they were acknowledging the needs of the congregation, the importance of caring for the widows, and the priority of the ministry of the apostles.

It is sometimes said that change is about unfreezing the system. Everything is liquid when change happens. It therefore becomes important to refreeze and, in a sense, this was what the apostles were doing. They brought closure to the dispute which had started the process and encouraged everyone to support those called to serve in this new initiative.

Bringing closure in this way doesn't mean the entire system is frozen. We are aiming to develop a culture of change, helping our congregations to see that change needs to be a constant feature of our maturing life as believers. We are to make progress as individuals and churches, 'straining towards what is ahead.' (Phil. 3: 13)

To return to the metaphor of the body, Paul reminds us where everything should be headed in the local church. He explains why the gifts of the ascended Christ are given, and perhaps this is the best passage with which to conclude both this chapter and this small book:

> . . . to equip his people for works of service, so that the body of
> Christ may be built up until we all reach unity in the faith and in
> the knowledge of the Son of God and become mature, attaining to
> the whole measure of the fullness of Christ.

Then we will no longer be infants, tossed back and forth by the waves, and blown here and there by every wind of teaching and by the cunning and craftiness of people in their deceitful scheming. Instead, speaking the truth in love, we will grow to become in every respect the mature body of him who is the head, that is, Christ. From him the whole body, joined and held together by every supporting ligament, grows and builds itself up in love, as each part does its work. (Ephesians 4: 12–16)

That is our goal. May the Lord give us grace to play our part.

DISCUSSION AND APPLICATION

1. *Take a look at each area of church life where change might be needed.*
   - What aspects of the approach of the apostles in Acts 6 might be particularly helpful to consider?

2. *To change or not to change?*
   - How does a local church determine what aspects of church life should not be changed, and what things must change in line with changing needs, circumstances, cultural realities, and expectations?

3. *We saw how the apostles were able to create a sense of ownership of the issue that needed to be managed.*
   - How might this best be done in your local church?

4. *One aspect of creating ownership is the need for transparency.*
   - In what ways can your local church create appropriate transparency, such that proposed changes do not come as a complete surprise to the congregation?

5. *The apostles in Acts 6 did a good job in delegating responsibilities.*
   - In what ways can we deploy the gifts of a wider cross-section of the members of our church?

Further Reading

John W. Baigent, *Building Biblical Churches* (Tiverton: Partnership, 2012)

D. A. Carson, *A Call to Spiritual Reformation* (Nottingham: IVP, 1992),

Sinclair B. Ferguson, *Maturity: Growing Up and Going On in the Christian Life* (Edinburgh: Banner of Truth, 2019)

Jonathan Lamb, *Essentially One: stiving for the unity God loves* (Nottingham: IVP, 2020)

Richard N. Longenecker (ed.), *Patterns of Discipleship in the New Testament* (Grand Rapids MI: Wm. B. Eerdmans, 1996)

J. I. Packer & Gary Parrett, *Grounded in the Gospel* (Grand Rapids MI: Baker Books, 2010)

John Stott, *The Living Church* (Nottingham: IVP, 2007)

Kevin Vanhoozer, *Hearers and Doers: A Pastor's Guide to Making Disciples Through Scripture and Doctrine* (London: Lexham Press, 2019)